Editors
Rebecca Wood
Erica N. Russikoff, M.A.

Illustrator
Mark Mason

Cover Artists
Kevin Barnes
Barb Lorseyedi

Editor in Chief
Ina Massler Levin, M.A.

Creative Director
Karen J. Goldfluss, M.S. Ed.

Art Coordinator
Renée Christine Yates

Imaging
Rosa C. See

Publisher
Mary D. Smith, M.S. Ed.

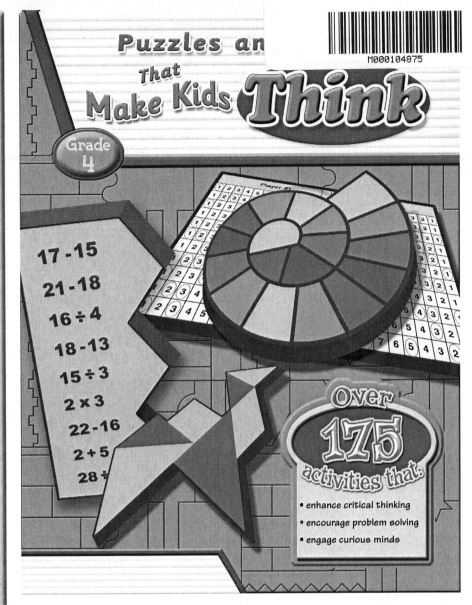

Author

Garth Sundem, M.M.

Teacher Created Resources, Inc.
6421 Industry Way
Westminster, CA 92683
www.teachercreated.com

ISBN: 978-1-4206-2564-6

©2009 Teacher Created Resources, Inc.
Reprinted, 2014
Made in U.S.A.

Table of Contents

Table of Contents (cont.)

Introduction

Welcome to *Puzzles and Games That Make Kids Think.* This book contains 190 puzzles and games of more than 30 different types, each of which is not only fun, but also asks students to use their minds to figure out the solution. (There are no "word finds" here!) Students will find some of these puzzles difficult, while other puzzles will be easy. Some puzzles will take seconds, while others might take half an hour. All of the puzzles are a workout for the brain! Here are a few reasons why we think you'll enjoy this book:

- Puzzle-based brain workouts create results. Research shows that a regimen of brainteasers can lead to higher scores on problem-solving tests.[1] Research also shows that using puzzles in the classroom can lead to increased student interest and involvement.[2]

- There are four categories of brainteasers in this book: picture, word, number, and logic, with puzzles (for individual students) and games (for pairs) for each category. Within each section, students will use diverse thinking skills—in a picture puzzle, students may draw lines on a geometric figure, and in a number puzzle, they may need to read complex directions. The wide variety of puzzles keeps students engaged and entertained.

- Each page of this book includes all of the needed directions and materials (other than writing utensils!), making it easy to distribute these puzzles to early finishers. Or, you may choose to copy and distribute puzzles as part of a reward system or weekly brain-buster challenge. Students will look forward to these fun puzzles, and you can rest assured that your classroom time will be spent productively. Another use of these puzzles is to spice up homework packets—strategically insert a puzzle or two to keep things lively!

- With a less experienced class, you may need to preview puzzle directions ahead of time (especially the two-person games and logic puzzles). Consider exploring the directions as a class before independent work time. Or, explain that reading and understanding the instructions is the first part of the puzzle! Because puzzle types repeat, students will gain more confidence in their ability to solve the puzzles as they spend more time with this book.

Be careful—these puzzles are addictive, and you can easily find yourself whiling away a prep period with pencil in hand!

[1] Howard, P. J. (1994). *The Owner's Manual for the Brain.* Charlotte, NC: Leornian Press.
[2] Finke, R. A., et al. (1992). *Creative Cognition: Theory, Research, and Applications.* Cambridge, MA: The MIT Press.

Puzzle Hints

Game Hints

Some games require the ability to read and understand somewhat difficult directions. Consider previewing directions with students beforehand. Also notice that some games require photocopying the page (or allowing students to cut shapes or game boards from the book). With less experienced classes, you might play a full-class version of a game (teacher versus students) before allowing pairs to work independently. In hopes of keeping game directions brief and student friendly, many of the more intuitive directions have been omitted. If students have questions about game mechanics, encourage them to use their common sense.

Picture Puzzles

- *Map Madness!:* Make sure you start at the correct point. Then, follow the route with your finger.
- *Rebus:* Where are words and/or pictures in relation to each other or to other elements? Say these relationships aloud and listen for common phrases.
- *Shape Find:* First, imagine the shape in your mind. Then, try to work around the figure systematically. And don't forget the whole figure itself!
- *Shape Slap:* Use the big shapes first. Place them in ways that will block your opponent.
- *Split Shapes:* Usually the lines are drawn from corners. Start there first.
- *Spun Shapes:* Imagine the first shape spun around the face of a clock. As it spins, which of the other shapes does it match? There is one shape that is different.
- *That's Not an Animal!:* Look for body parts borrowed from another animal (e.g., a hippo with antlers).
- *What's Different?:* Pretend there is a grid over each picture, and confine your search to only one box at a time.

Word Puzzles

- *Before and After:* If it doesn't come to you right away, brainstorm animals that would fit the correct number of boxes.
- *Changing Letters:* Pick the letter that you're going to try to change. If you can't think of something right away, scroll through the alphabet to see what fits. Think about *A*, then *B*, then *C*, then *D,* and go until something works.
- *Crack the Code:* Fill in each box in order. If you're running out of time, you can usually guess the answer before finishing the last few boxes.
- *Crossword:* Do the easy ones first. Then, use those letters to help you determine the more difficult ones.
- *Crossword Challenge*: The only way to do this is to guess and check. Start by adding the first word wherever you can, and then try to make the rest fit. Write lightly in pencil in case you have to erase the words and start again!
- *Hide and Seek:* Scan the sentence slowly, looking for the names of different animals.
- *Letter Scramble:* Play with the vowel—it's usually the key.
- *Missing Letter:* Try the missing letter in every position, starting at the front and working your way through the word.
- *Rhyme Game:* Try replacing the first letter of a word with another letter. Go through the entire alphabet until you find a word that rhymes.

Puzzle Hints *(cont.)*

Word Puzzles *(cont.)*

- *Transformers:* Look at the last word. What letter from this word could be inserted in the first word to make a new word? Repeat until you get to the bottom.

- *Word Circles:* Most words start next to the vowel. Look there first.

Number Puzzles

- *Fill in the Blanks:* Start on the right, with the singles digit, and then work left.

- *In Addition:* If there are three numbers in any row or column, you can find the fourth number. Do those first.

- *It's Touching:* First, look for rows or columns that are missing only one number. Then, look for shaded numbers with only one blank box touching.

- *Math Path:* You will almost always add the greatest numbers. In longer puzzles, look for a path between the two greatest numbers that includes an addition sign for both.

- *Operation Box:* Think of it in chunks, with two numbers and an equal sign. Fill in "chunks" with only one missing piece. Remember, there are no negatives!

- *Snake Race:* Keep in mind the numbers that add up to your target number. Then, look for one of those numbers in the puzzle. Start at that number and experiment with ways to move until you find the combination you need.

- *Sudoku:* If a row, column, or 2 x 2 box already contains three numbers, you can fill in the fourth. Fill those in before proceeding.

- *Thinking of a Number:* Work from the filled-in digit, if there is one.

- *Tic-Tac-Toe Race:* Scan for the easiest problems. Complete those first. Don't waste time trying to block your opponent. Just go for the win as fast as you can!

Logic Puzzles

- *Adam's Coat, Liza's Magic Wand, etc.:* Memorize the three things you are looking for (e.g., + star, - stripes, + long). Then scan the puzzle in order, looking for the picture that matches the description.

- *How Old?:* There are two things that have to be true. Try to figure out the first true thing, and then experiment with numbers that would also make the second thing true.

- *Letter Box:* You will need to know the definitions of *row* and *column* to solve these.

- *Miguel, Anna, Tran, and Lisa:* If three people did not do something, the fourth must have. If someone did something, it means that no one else did it and that he or she did not do anything else. (This will help you draw **X**s on the chart).

- *Odd Animal Out:* Think about starting letters, or look for things that three of the animals have in common. Maybe there's more than one answer!

- *What's Next?:* Look for the repeating pattern.

Shape Find

1

How many triangles can you find in this picture? 4 _____

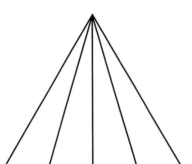

Spun Shapes

2

Which one of the shapes is not like the others? Circle it.

That's Not an Animal!

3

Put an **X** through the animal that is not real.

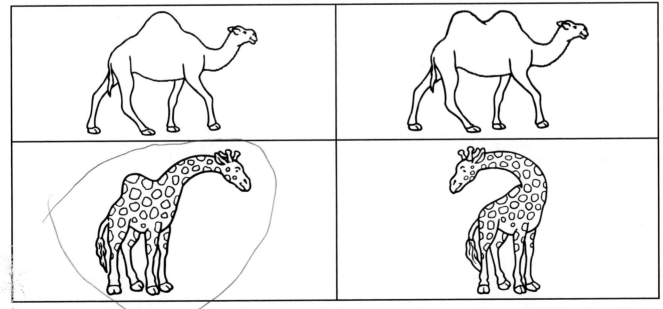

Rebus

4

These are pictures of common sayings. What are they?

knock
WOOD

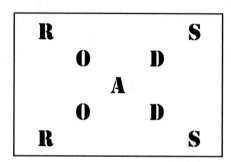

_____   _____

What's Different?

5

Can you spot the five differences between these two pictures. Circle them.

Crayon Game

6

Directions:

1. Put a red, blue, and green crayon in a bag, hat, or box.
2. Find a partner, and choose who goes first.
3. Pick a crayon from the bag. Don't peek!
4. Go to the next space on the board with that color. Color in that space. This space is now blocked. If the next space on the board is already colored in (blocked), you can't land there, and you miss your turn. (If all of the "next" spaces in front of you are blocked, then you lose!)
5. Put the crayon back in the bag, hat, or box.
6. Take turns picking crayons until one of you reaches "FINISH." If you pick the same color twice in a row, go back to "START."
7. For the last move, stay at your spot until you pick the ending color. Again, if you get the same one twice in a row, go back to the beginning.

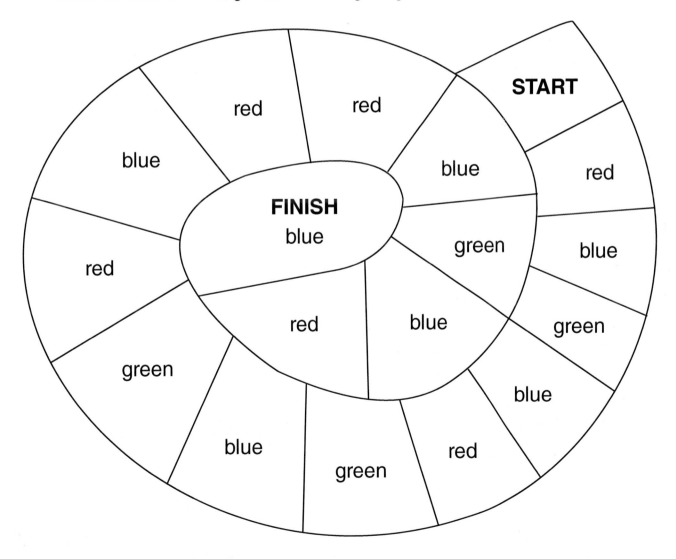

Map Madness!

7

Do you see Pedro? He is lost! Follow the directions to get him back on track. Mark his ending spot with an **X**.

Directions:

1. ← Go west on Garfield St.

2. ↓ Go south on Kelsey Ave.

3. → Go east on Jefferson St.

4. ↑ Go north on Karen Ave.

5. ← Go west on Madison St.

6. **END** End at the corner of Alice Ave.

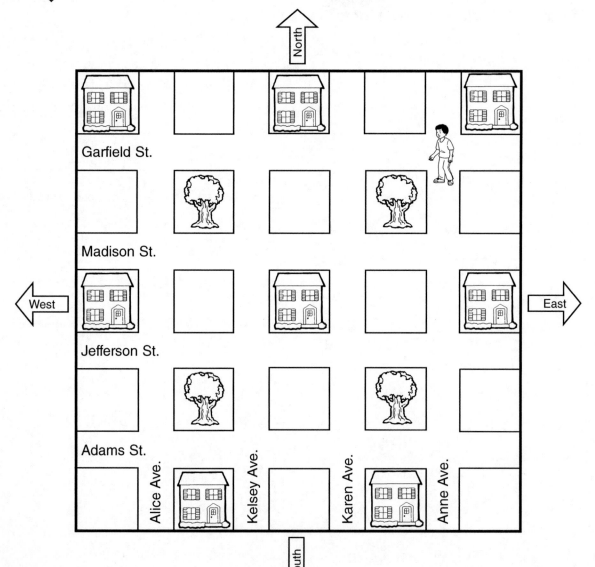

Split Shapes

8

Can you draw six lines on this shape to make twelve triangles?

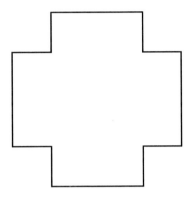

What's Different?

9

Can you spot the five differences between these two pictures? Circle them.

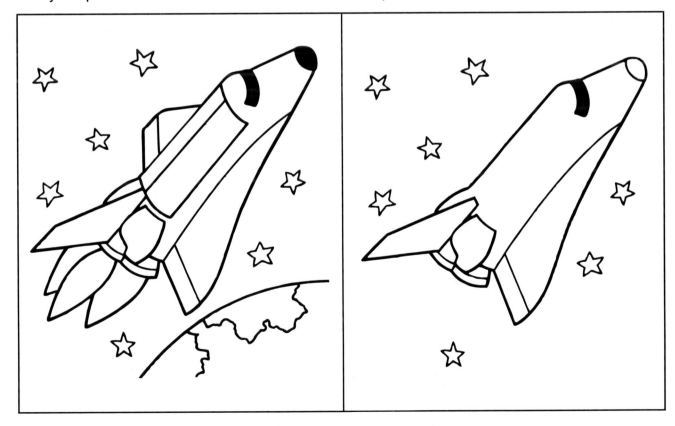

Picture Puzzles

Brainstorm Game

Directions:

1. Find a partner. Then, look at the object on the right.

2. It is a fishing pole, but what else could it be?

3. You have 30 seconds to write one thing it could be on your set of lines. Be creative!

4. Now, it is your partner's turn.

5. Keep going until one person takes more than 30 seconds. The other person is the winner!

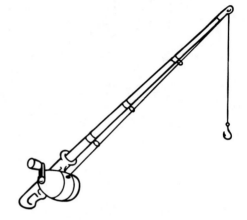

Player #1	Player #2
_____	_____
_____	_____
_____	_____
_____	_____
_____	_____
_____	_____
_____	_____
_____	_____
_____	_____

12   ©*Teacher Created Resources, Inc.*

Map Madness!

11

Do you see Pedro? He is lost again! Follow the directions to get him back on track. Mark his ending spot with an **X**.

Directions:

1. ⬆ Go north on Aardvark Ave. 4. ➡ Go east on Art St.

2. ⬅ Go west on Armor St. 5. ⬆ Go north on Alligator Ave.

3. ⬇ Go south on Armadillo Ave. 6. **END** End at the corner of Apple St.

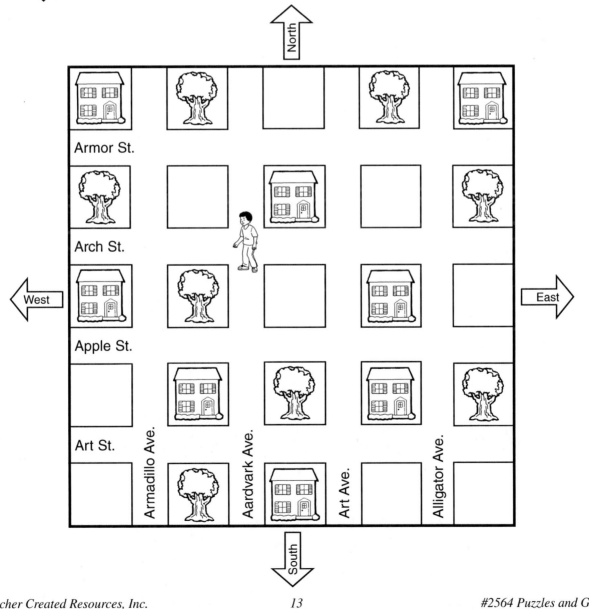

That's Not an Animal!

12

Put an **X** through the animal that is not real.

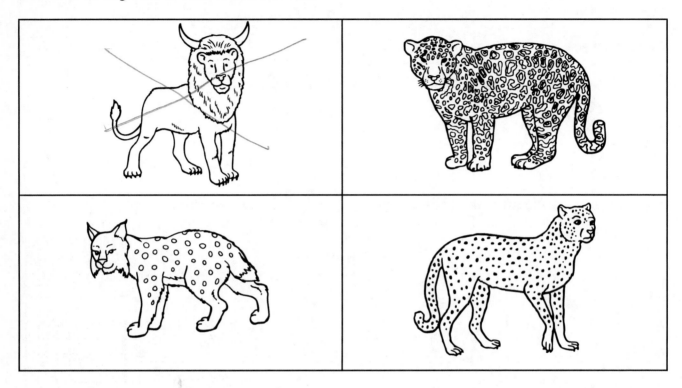

What's Different?

13

Can you spot the five differences between these two pictures? Circle them.

Shape Slap

14

Directions:

1. Find a partner. Look at the game board. Then, look at the shapes.
2. Pick a shape. Color in this shape on the board. If you need to, you can spin the shape. Draw an **X** over the shape you used.
3. Now, it is your partner's turn.
4. The first person who does not have room to place a shape loses!

Shapes:

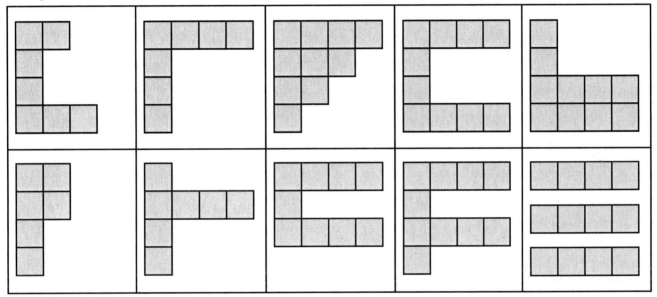

Game Board:

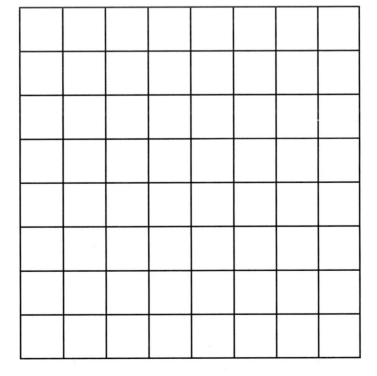

Spun Shapes

15

Which one of these shapes is not like the others? Circle it.

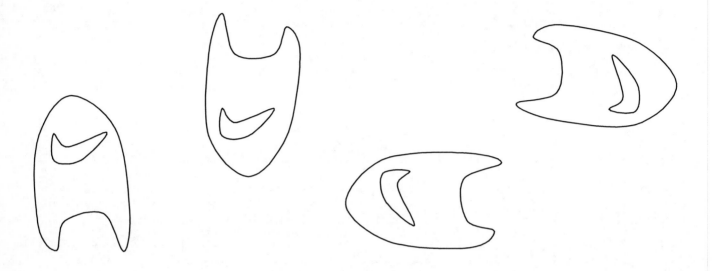

Shape Find

16

Try this tricky challenge! How many rectangles can you find in this picture? _____

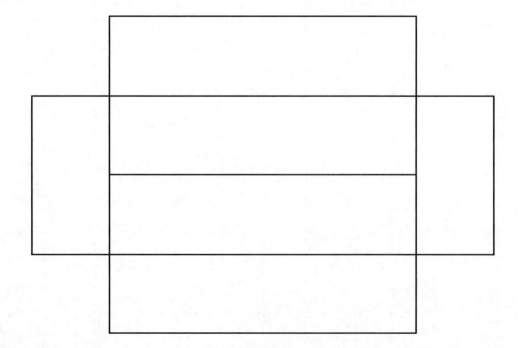

17 Split Shapes

Can you draw another triangle on this shape to make five new triangles and one pentagon (five sides)?

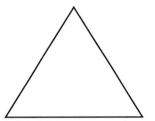

18 Rebus

These are pictures of common sayings. What are they?

Read	thou*deep*ght

_____   _____

19 That's Not an Animal!

Put an **X** through the animal that is not real.

Tangram Game

Directions:

1. Find a partner. Each of you will need a copy of this sheet with your own set of shapes. Cut out the shapes in the square below.
2. Look at the tangram pictures below. When you say "go," you and your partner will race to make these pictures using all of your shapes.
3. Once one of you has made a picture, cross it out. This picture is now used. Both you and your partner should move on to the next picture.
4. Whoever makes the most pictures wins!

Shapes:

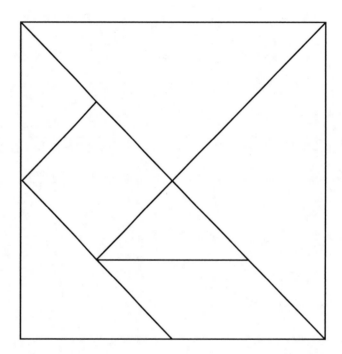

Tangram Pictures:

Map Madness!

21

Do you see Pedro? He is lost again! Follow the directions to get him back on track. Mark his ending spot with an **X**.

Directions:

1. ➡️ Go east on Block St.

2. ⬆️ Go north on Drag Ave.

3. ➡️ Go east on Back St.

4. ⬆️ Go north on Drip Ave.

5. ⬅️ Go west on Black St.

6. **END** End at the corner of Dog Ave.

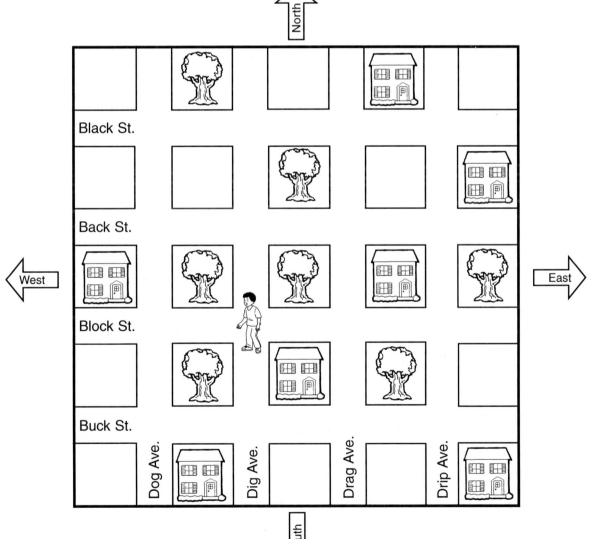

Shape Find

22

Try this tricky challenge! How many triangles can you find in this picture? _____

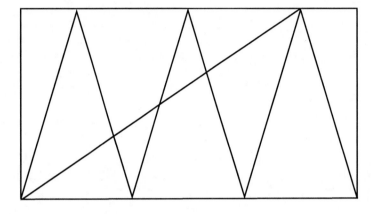

What's Different?

23

Can you spot the five differences between these two pictures? Circle them.

Cartoon Helpers

24

Directions:

1. Find a partner. You will each need a pencil.

2. Look at the boxes below. The first box shows the start of a cartoon.

3. Draw the next box. Then, have your partner write the caption for what you drew. Don't talk!

4. Now you will trade jobs: Your partner will draw the next box, and you will write the caption.

5. Take turns until all of the boxes are filled in.

6. At the end, work together to tell the complete story.

Pictures			
Captions	Peter and Anna are flying a kite.		

Pictures			
Captions			

Split Shapes

25

Can you draw one line on this shape to make four new triangles and two rectangles?

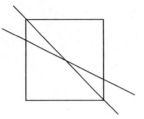

Rebus

26

These are pictures of common sayings. What are they?

Jack		wear long

_____   _____

That's Not an Animal!

27

Put an **X** through the animal that is not real.

Map Madness!

Do you see Pedro? He is lost again! Follow the directions to get him back on track. Mark his ending spot with an **X**.

Directions:

1. Go south on Yellow Ave.

2. Go east on Red St.

3. Go north on Orange Ave.

4. Go west on Pink St.

5. Go south on Purple Ave.

6. **END** End at the corner of Green St.

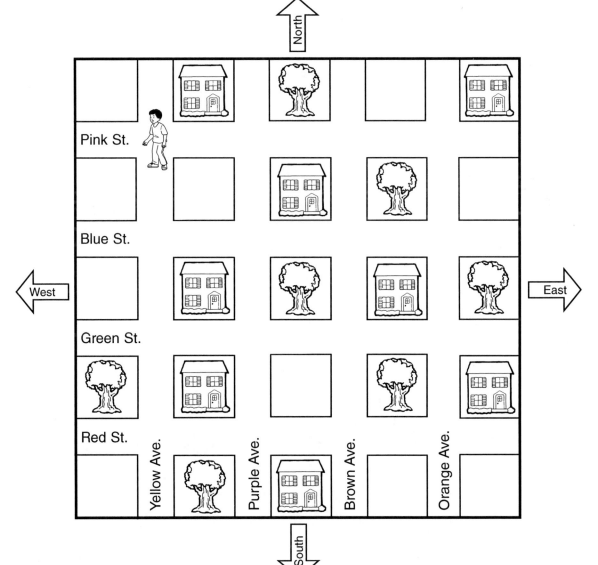

Triangle Take-Away Game

Directions:

1. Find a partner.

2. Put a blank piece of paper over the picture below, and trace it lightly in pencil.

3. Take turns erasing a line. You can erase a long or short line. But, you must leave at least one triangle.

4. The first person who cannot leave a triangle loses.

5. If you have time, trace the shape again and play another round!

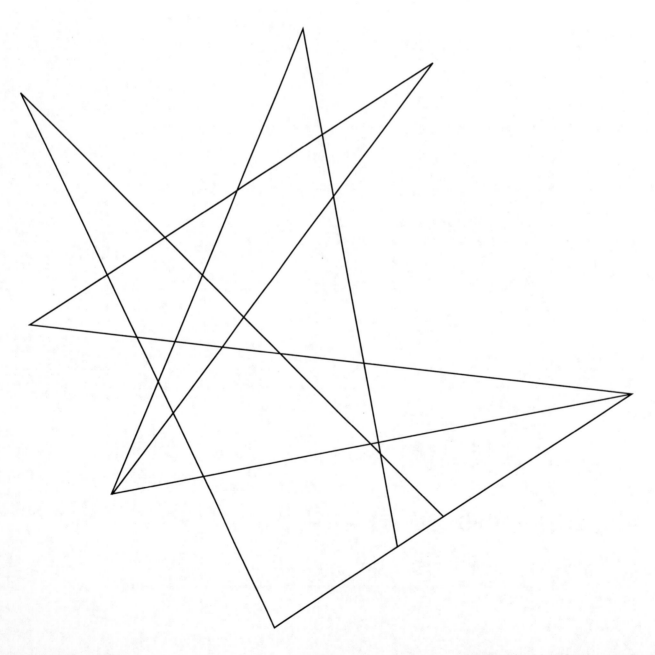

Spun Shapes

30

Which one of these shapes is not like the others? Circle it.

 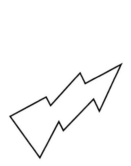  

Shape Find

31

Try this tricky challenge! How many triangles can you find in this picture? _____

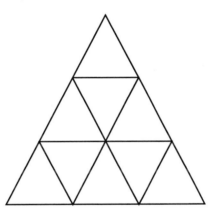

Rebus

32

These are pictures of common sayings. What are they?

_____   _____

Split Shapes

33

Try this tricky challenge! Can you draw another square on this shape to make twelve new triangles? You will have to draw in the shaded area. Consider using a ruler.

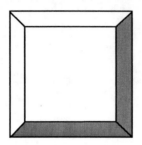

That's Not an Animal!

34

Put an **X** through the animal that is not real.

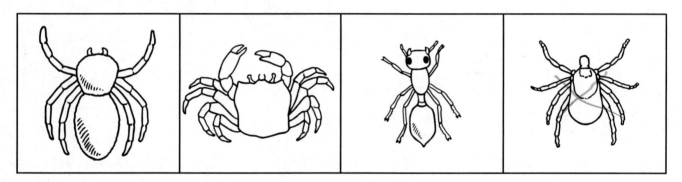

What's Different?

35

Can you spot the five differences between these two pictures? Circle them.

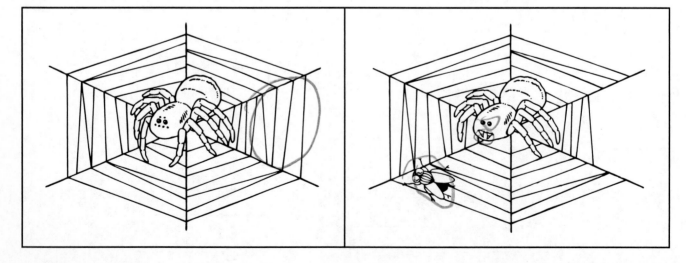

Shape Slap

36

Directions:

1. Find a partner. Look at the game board. Then, look at the shapes.
2. Pick a shape. Color in this shape on the board. If you need to, you can spin the shape. Draw an **X** over the shape you used.
3. Now, it is your partner's turn.
4. The first person who does not have room to place a shape loses!

Shapes:

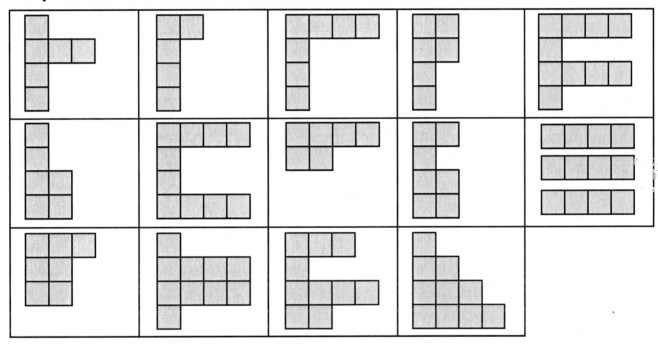

Game Board:

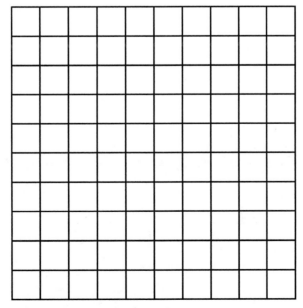

Map Madness!

Try this tricky challenge—without direction words! Do you see Pedro? He is lost again!
Follow the directions to get him back on track. Mark his ending spot with an **X**.

Directions:

1. Take Wolf St. to Sparrow Ct.

2. Take Sparrow Ct. to Dingo St.

3. Take Dingo St. to East Finch Ave.

4. Take East Finch Ave. to Fox St.

5. Take Fox St. toward West Finch Ave.

6. **END** End at the corner of Robin Ln.

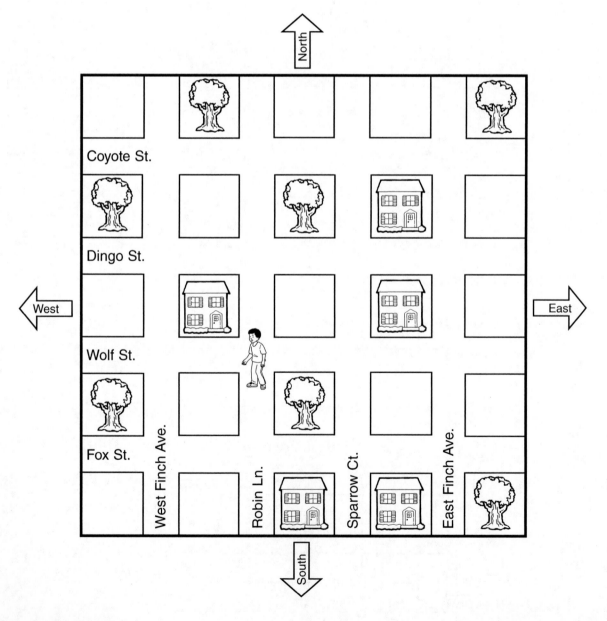

Picture Puzzles

Spun Shapes
38

Which one of these shapes is not like the others? Circle it.

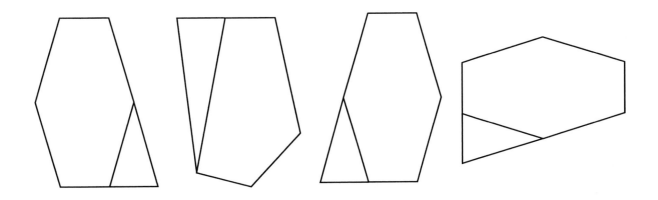

Shape Find
39

Try this tricky challenge! How many triangles can you find in this picture? _____

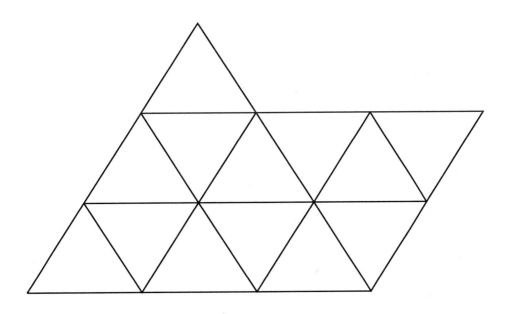

Missing Letter
40

The letter "p" has been taken out of the front, middle, or end of these words. The letter might be used more than once. What are the words?

en: _____   oen: _____

jum: _____   lan: _____

um: _____, _____   imossible: _____

lum: _____, _____ , _____

Transformers
41

Change one letter at a time to get from the top word to the bottom word. Each row must make a real word.

Example:

p	e	s	t
p	**o**	s	t
p	o	**e**	t
p	o	e	**m**

b	r	a	g
n	e	a	t

Crossword
42

Read the clues and fill in the letters.

Across

1. I _____ about the environment.
5. the opposite of *closed*
6. The teacher _____ a story.
7. makes a mistake

Down

1. the center of an apple
2. one who apes (copies)
3. the back
4. All stories have beginnings and _____.

1	2	3	4
5			
6			
7			

Hide and Seek
43

Can you find the three animals hiding in this sentence? Circle them.

Example: Help igloos!

The bowl's crunchy enamel was enough to anger Bill.

Crack the Code
44

What type of person loves to drink hot chocolate? Crack the code to find out!

u	c	t	n	a	o
1	2	3	4	5	6

	■							
5		2	6	2	6	4	1	3

Word Circles
45

Start at any letter. Go left or right. What fruits can you spell? Write them in the circles.

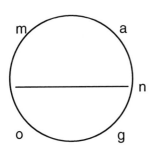

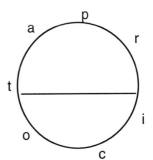

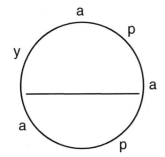

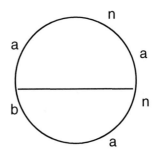

Crossword Challenge

46

Directions:

1. Using different-colored pens, work with a partner to put these words into the crossword puzzle. Each word must touch at least one other word.

2. Now, take turns adding new words to the puzzle. Be creative!

3. The person who can add the most new words wins.

bear   zebra

horse   birdie   deer

		L	I	Z	A	R	D		

#2564 Puzzles and Games   32   *©Teacher Created Resources, Inc.*

Word Puzzles

47 Letter Scramble

Make three words using all of these letters: rtsa.

1. _____

2. _____

3. _____

Now, use the words to write a sentence about the picture.

_____

_____

48 Hide and Seek

Can you find the three animals hiding in this sentence? Circle them.

Example: Help igloos!

Common keywords to realize Brazil are rainfall, Amazon, and soccer.

49 Crossword

Read the clues and fill in the letters.

Across

1. You do it with a mixing spoon.
5. a game: _____ and seek
6. the opposite of *closed*
7. what you might whisper to get someone's attention

Down

1. a place to buy things
2. the ends of your fingers
3. the _____ of March (*Hint:* starts with an "i")
4. to pay money to use something (like an apartment)

1	2	3	4
5			
6			
7			

50   Crack the Code

What animal keeps the best time? Crack the code to find out!

c	t	h	w	g	a	o	d
1	2	3	4	5	6	7	8

6	■	4	6	2	1	3	8	7	5

51   Transformers

Change one letter at a time to get from the top word to the bottom word. Each row must make a real word.

Example:

p	e	s	t
p	**o**	s	t
p	o	**e**	t
p	o	e	**m**

d	o	g	s
t	o	y	s

52   Letter Scramble

Make three words using all of these letters: wtse.

1. _____

2. _____

3. _____

Now, use the words to write a sentence about the picture.

_____

_____

Changing Letters

53

Directions:

1. Find a partner. Start with the word below.

2. Change one letter to make a new word. Write this word in the next row.

3. Take turns. You cannot use a word more than once.

4. If you cannot make a new word, you are out. When you reach the end of the puzzle together, you both win!

Example:

p	e	s	t
p	**o**	s	t
p	o	**e**	t
p	o	e	**m**

Start	h	o	s	e
1.				
2.				
3.				
4.				
5.				
6.				
7.				
8.				
9.				
10.				

Hide and Seek
54

Can you find the three animals hiding in this sentence? Circle them.

Example: Help igloos!

The okapi ran hard and tried to grab bits of food.

Word Circles
55

Start at any letter. Go left or right. What vegetables can you spell? Write them in the circles.

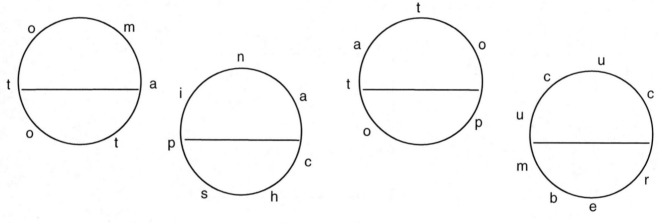

Crossword
56

Read the clues and fill in the letters.

Across
1. It comes from cows.
5. what you do to flatten clothes
6. a river in Egypt
7. another word for *island*

Down
1. small, as in a van
2. the center part of your eye
   (*Hint:* the third letter is "i")
3. to lay around lazily
4. a joint in your leg

1	2	3	4
5			
6			
7			

Transformers

57

Change one letter at a time to get from the top word to the bottom word. Each row must make a real word.

Example:

p	e	s	t
p	**o**	s	t
p	o	**e**	t
p	o	e	**m**

s	l	e	d
b	e	n	d

Word Circles

58

Start at any letter. Go left or right. What desserts can you spell? Write them in the circles.

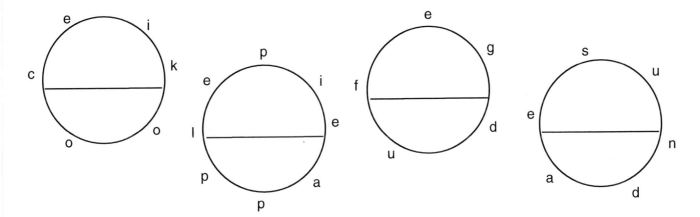

Crack the Code

59

What belongs to you but is used more by others? Crack the code to find out!

e	r	o	a	y	u	n	m
1	2	3	4	5	6	7	8

				■			
5	3	6	2		7	4	8	1

Fronts and Backs

60

Directions:

1. These letters are the "fronts" and "backs" of words.

2. Find a partner. Make a word using the "fronts" and "backs" provided. Write it in your space.

3. Take turns writing words.

4. If you cannot make a new word, you are out.

5. The person with the most words wins!

Fronts	Backs
beg	inning
w	ell
sp	ency
ag	ain
anci	ent
pal	ace
emerg	
br	
effici	

Player #1	Player #2

Crossword
61

Read the clues and fill in the letters.

Across

1. Have you _____ the school play?
5. to walk back and forth
6. a muscle pain
7. a horse that has been fixed with shoes

Down

1. hot tubs
2. There is enough for _____ of you.
3. It talks back to you in a canyon.
4. more than a want, it's a _____

1	2	3	4
5			
6			
7			

Hide and Seek
62

Can you find the three animals hiding in this sentence? Circle them.

Example: Help igloos!

My grandmother feels you should always capitalize Brandon.

Letter Scramble
63

Make three words using all of these letters: ispt.

1. _____
2. _____
3. _____

Now, use the words to write a sentence about the picture.

_____

_____

Missing Letter
64

The letter "s" has been taken out of the front, middle, or end of these words. The letter might be used more than once. Adding an "s" to a word you already found doesn't count! What are the words?

un: _____   hoe: _____ , _____ , _____

upene: _____   lip: _____ , _____

miiippi: _____

plah: _____

Word Circles
65

Start at any letter. Go left or right. What flowers can you spell? Write them in the circles.

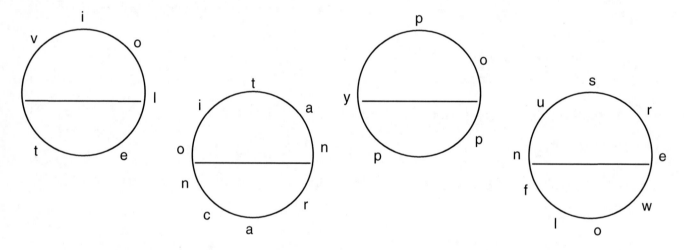

Crack the Code
66

Who is Dracula's favorite person on a baseball team? Crack the code to find out!

b	y	h	a	e	t	o
1	2	3	4	5	6	7

6	3	5	■	1	4	6	■	1	7	2

Beginnings and Ends Game

67

Directions:

1. Find a partner.

2. Look at the pictures below. Think of the words they show.

3. Start at *car*. This word ends with the letter "r." Which word begins with the letter "r"? The first one has been done for you.

4. Take turns drawing arrows to the next picture. Also, write the words you use.

5. If you cannot find a word in 30 seconds, your partner wins. If you can use every picture, you both win!

car

rat

Hide and Seek

68

Can you find the four animals hiding in this sentence? Circle them.

Example: Help igloos!

The scowling wizards' wands made the limo useless.

Before and After

69

Put an animal name in the blank boxes so that it makes a word or short phrase with the word in front and the word after.

Example:

| S | P | E | L | L | I | N | G | | | H | I | V | E | = SPELLING BEE HIVE |

| T | O | M | | | | N | A | P |

Crossword

70

Read the clues and fill in the letters.

Across

1. this and _____

5. the tortoise and the _____

6. _____ and odd

7. the opposite of *messy*

Down

1. now and _____

2. _____ and have not

3. another word for *space*

4. You sleep in it when you go camping.

1	2	3	4
5			
6			
7			

Crack the Code

71

What kind of house weighs the least? Crack the code to find out!

g	l	h	t	i	o	a	e	u	s
1	2	3	4	5	6	7	8	9	10

7	■	2	5	1	3	4	3	6	9	10	8

Letter Scramble

72

Make three words using all of these letters: badre.

1. _____

2. _____

3. _____

Now, use the words to write a sentence about the picture.

_____

_____

Word Circles

73

Start at any letter. Go left or right. What geographic features can you spell? Write them in the circles.

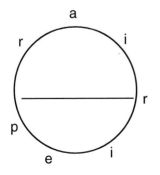
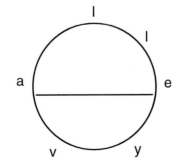
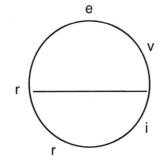
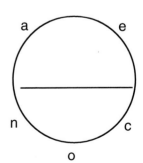

74 Missing Letter

The letter "t" has been taken out of the front, middle, or end of these words. The letter might be used more than once. What are the words?

poao: _____   rap:_____ , _____

oer: _____   ha: _____ , _____

wich:_____ , _____   sar: _____ , _____

75 Rhyme Game

Directions:

1. Find a partner. Each player should use a different-colored pen. Then, look at the words below.
2. Race your partner to write rhymes for these words. Remember, words don't have to be spelled the same in order to rhyme!
3. Once you write a rhyme in a box, the box is closed.
4. Whoever closes the most boxes wins!
5. If you have time, work together to write a poem using some of these words.

clown	flower	chicken
_____ rhyme	_____ rhyme	_____ rhyme
fast	coat	bicycle
_____ rhyme	_____ rhyme	_____ rhyme
space	wand	proud
_____ rhyme	_____ rhyme	_____ rhyme
math	noodle	crumpet
_____ rhyme	_____ rhyme	_____ rhyme

76 Transformers

Change one letter at a time to get from the top word to the bottom word. Each row must make a real word.

Example:

p	e	s	t
p	**o**	s	t
p	o	**e**	t
p	o	e	**m**

m	i	s	t
h	o	s	e

77 Before and After

Put an animal name in the blank boxes so that it makes a word or short phrase with the word in front and the word after.

Example:

| S | P | E | L | L | I | N | G | | | H | I | V | E | = SPELLING BEE HIVE |

| U | N | D | E | R | | | D | A | Y | S |

78 Missing Letter

The letter "a" has been taken out of the front, middle, or end of these words. The letter might be used more than once. What are the words?

pln: _____

set: _____

mst: _____

rdvrk: _____

pe: _____ , _____

re: _____ , _____

sp: _____ , _____ , _____

Crossword

79

Read the clues and fill in the letters.

Across

1. another name for a boat
5. a game: _____ and seek
6. space
7. how you begin a letter

Down

1. a type of fish (This one is tricky!)
2. to pay somebody to do a job
3. I have an _____ !
4. a type of fruit: not a plum, but a _____

1	2	3	4
5			
6			
7			

Before and After

80

Put an animal name in the blank boxes so that it makes a word or short phrase with the word in front and the word after.

Example:

S	P	E	L	L	I	N	G				H	I	V	E	= SPELLING BEE HIVE

O	U	T				T	A	I	L

Word Circles

81

Start at any letter. Go left or right. What games can you spell? Write them in the circles.

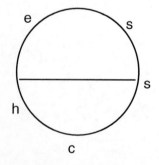
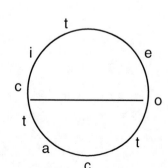
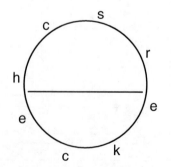
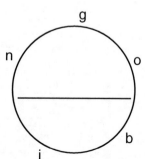

Crossword Challenge

82

Directions:

1. Using different-colored pens, work with a partner to put these words into the crossword puzzle. Each word must touch at least one other word.

2. Now, take turns adding new words to the puzzle. Be creative!

3. The person who can add the most new words wins.

4. Once you have finished the game, write clues for your answers. Make a crossword board with numbers that match your answers. Ask a friend to solve your crossword puzzle!

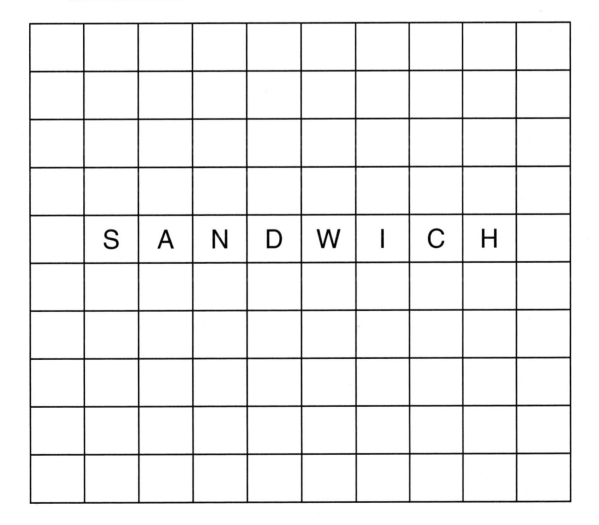

Transformers

83

Change one letter at a time to get from the top word to the bottom word. Each row must make a real word.

Example:

p	e	s	t
p	**o**	s	t
p	o	**e**	t
p	o	e	**m**

p	a	c	k
l	i	c	e

Hide and Seek

84

Can you find the four animals hiding in this sentence? Circle them.

Example: Help igloos!

The flea gleefully came late to the blob's term party.

Crossword

85

Read the clues and fill in the letters.

Across

1. May the _____ runner win the race!
5. a buttery sandwich spread (This one is hard!)
6. abbreviation: As Soon As Possible
7. Toy trains come in 100-piece _____.

Down

1. snakes that coil around their victims
2. Sit down or _____ !
3. That's right, have a _____ !
4. the opposite of *bottoms*

1	2	3	4
5			
6			
7			

48

Missing Letter
86

The letter "c" has been taken out of the front, middle, or end of these words. The letter might be used more than once. What are the words?

ae: _____   speeh: _____

rouh: _____   raker: _____

at: _____ , _____   hithat: _____

Before and After
87

Put an animal name in the blank boxes so that it makes a word or short phrase with the word in front and the word after.

Example:

| S | P | E | L | L | I | N | G | | | | H | I | V | E |

= SPELLING BEE HIVE

| | S | U | N | | | | B | O | W | L |

Transformers
88

Change one letter at a time to get from the top word to the bottom word. Each row must make a real word.

Example:

p	e	s	t
p	**o**	s	t
p	o	**e**	t
p	o	e	**m**

o	p	e	n
e	v	e	r

Changing Letters

89

Directions:

1. Find a partner. Start with the word below.

2. Change one letter to make a new word. Write this word in the next row.

3. Take turns. You cannot use a word more than once.

4. If you cannot make a new word, you are out. If you reach the end of the puzzle, keep going. Use the back of this page if you need to.

Example:

p	e	s	t
p	o	s	t
p	o	e	t
p	o	e	m

Start	f	o	l	d
1.				
2.				
3.				
4.				
5.				
6.				
7.				
8.				
9.				
10.				

Missing Letter

90

The letter "g" has been taken out of the front, middle, or end of these words. The letter might be used more than once. What are the words?

ran:_____   urle: _____

lobe: _____   irl: _____

ore:_____ , _____   jule: _____

Crack the Code

91

What goes up a chimney down, but won't go down a chimney up? Crack the code to find out!

l	m	a	b	n	u	r	e
1	2	3	4	5	6	7	8

3	5	■	6	2	4	7	8	1	1	3

Word Circles

92

Start at any letter. Go left or right. What stores can you spell? Write them in the circles.

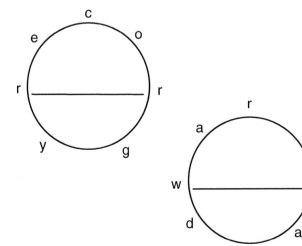

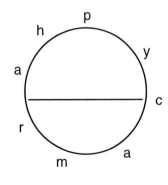

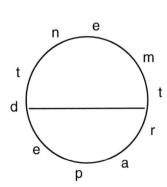

93   Before and After

Put an animal name in the blank boxes so that it makes a word or short phrase with the word in front and the word after.

Example:

| S | P | E | L | L | I | N | G | | | | H | I | V | E | = SPELLING BEE HIVE |

| E | A | R | T | H | | | | H | O | L | E |

94   Hide and Seek

Can you find the same animal two times in this sentence? Circle it each time.

Example: Help igloos!

I'll have the proposal Monday for the universal money.

95   Crossword

Read the clues and fill in the letters.

Across

1. the opposite of *open*
5. Water comes out of it.
6. the opposite of *shut*
7. Did you study for the _____ today?

Down

1. The circus acrobat _____ out of the cannon.
2. I _____ I did well on the quiz.
3. The carpenter always _____ a hammer.
4. You sleep in it when you go camping.

1	2	3	4
5			
6			
7			

Rhyme Game

96

Directions:

1. Find a partner. Each player should use a different-colored pen. Then, look at the words below.

2. Race your partner to write rhymes for these words. Remember, words don't have to be spelled the same in order to rhyme!

3. Once you write a rhyme in a box, the box is closed.

4. Whoever closes the most boxes wins!

5. If you have time, work together to write a poem using some of these words.

finger	mast	sleeping
_____ rhyme	_____ rhyme	_____ rhyme
barely	thing	choose
_____ rhyme	_____ rhyme	_____ rhyme
chose	wander	change
_____ rhyme	_____ rhyme	_____ rhyme
heavy	smelly	cheese
_____ rhyme	_____ rhyme	_____ rhyme

97 Crack the Code

I'm as small as an ant or as big as a whale. I'm as fast as a cheetah or as slow as a snail. On a sunny day, I'm always at your feet. What am I? Crack the code to find out!

h	d	a	s	w	o
1	2	3	4	5	6

3	■	4	1	3	2	6	5

98 Word Circles

Start at any letter. Go left or right. What words from the kitchen can you spell? Write them in the circles.

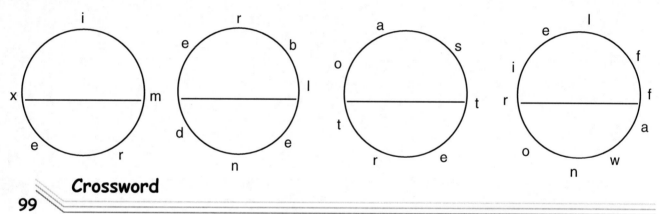

99 Crossword

Read the clues and fill in the letters.

Across

1. Your little sister can be one.
5. the opposite of *under*
6. a demonstration, for short
7. If you are in a bad mood, you are in a _____ . (This one is tricky!)

Down

1. Peas are in them.
2. Numbers are either this, or they are odd.
3. a type of truck
4. slower than a gallop

1	2	3	4
5			
6			
7			

Before and After
100

Put an animal name in the blank boxes so that it makes a word or short phrase with the letters in front and the letters after.

Example:

S	P	E	L	L	I	N	G			H	I	V	E

= SPELLING BEE HIVE

S	T	O	O	L						T	O	E	D

Transformers
101

Change one letter at a time to get from the top word to the bottom word. Each row must make a real word.

Example:

p	e	s	t
p	**o**	s	t
p	o	**e**	t
p	o	e	**m**

m	o	o	n
c	o	l	d

Crossword
102

Read the clues and fill in the letters.

Across

1. Are you _____ to do it?
5. to give, expecting it back (*Hint:* not *lend*)
6. moved, as on a sled
7. You use them to paddle a boat.

Down

1. I _____ like to ski.
2. a type of necktie (*Hint:* It's one letter away from a type of snake.)
3. where a dragon lives (*Hint:* not a *cave*)
4. the opposite of *begins*

1	2	3	4
5			
6			
7			

In Addition
103

Fill in the blanks with the digits 1–9 so that the sum of each row is the number to the right, and the sum of each column is the number below it.

		8	12
4	2		15
8			19

15	7	24

Math Path
104

Pick the best starting number, and then go up/down or left/right until you have touched all of the spaces once. What is the *highest* total you can end with? Draw your path.

2	+	6
–	4	+
5	–	7

Total: _____

Number Puzzles

Each row, column, and 2 x 2 box has the digits 1, 2, 3, and 4. Fill in the blanks to complete the puzzle.

2	3	4	
4		2	3
1	2		4
	4	1	2

In Addition
106

Fill in the blanks with the digits 1–9 so that the sum of each row is the number to the right, and the sum of each column is the number below it.

	2	5	6	18
4	6		6	25
2				13
		7	2	16
12	18	23	19	

Tic-Tac-Toe Race

107

Directions:

1. Pick a colored pen. Have your partner pick a different color.

2. Choose a tic-tac-toe board, and sit side by side.

3. Start at the same time, and race to solve the math problems.

4. When you solve a problem, write the answer in the box.

5. If you get three in a row, you win!

6. Check your answers. If your partner wrote a wrong answer, the space is yours!

Example:

6 – 4	4 + 2	8 – 3
9 + 5 14	4 + 5	2 + 7
1 + 6	3 + 9	7 – 5

Game Boards:

6 x 4	8 x 9	32 – 17
54 + 31	47 – 39	5 x 8
86 – 38	7 x 6	23 + 48

48 + 34	75 – 27	3 x 9
3 + 2	4 x 9	33 + 29
9 x 5	35 + 73	52 – 33

64 – 45	7 x 7	16 + 62
8 x 9	98 – 89	39 + 49
12 + 89	8 x 6	37 – 18

34 – 17	4 x 7	47 – 34
5 x 5	7 x 3	45 – 44
6 x 9	54 + 47	33 + 29

Number Puzzles

Math Path
108

Pick the best starting number, and then go up/down or left/right until you have touched all of the spaces once. What is the *highest* total you can end with? Draw your path.

2	+	6
–	3	+
1	–	1

Total: _____

Thinking of a Number
109

I'm thinking of a four-digit number in which:

- the third digit is the product of the first and second.
- the first and second digits are consecutive numbers, and the first digit is not a one.
- the last digit is the sum of the second and third digits.

Operation Box
110

Fill in each blank box with a number so that everything that touches is true and positive.

			=	
=		+		
6		3		7
–				=
4	=		+	

111 Sudoku

Each row, column, and 2 x 2 box has the digits 1, 2, 3, and 4. Fill in the blanks to complete the puzzle.

1			2
4	2	1	3
2	1	3	4
3			1

112 In Addition

Fill in the blanks with the digits 1–9 so that the sum of each row is the number to the right, and the sum of each column is the number below it.

4		4	17
	6	7	18
			12

12	16	19

Snake Race

Directions:

1. Find a partner. Each player should use a different-colored pen.

2. Sit side by side, and put the game board in front of you.

3. Look for snakes that add up to twenty-one. The numbers have to be touching. (You cannot jump around.) Once a number is taken, you cannot use it again.

4. Take turns. You have 30 seconds to find a snake.

5. If you cannot find a snake in 30 seconds, the other person wins.

Example:

5	+	4	+
+	8	+	12
7	+	6	+
+	6	+	9

Game Board:

14	+	3	+	1	+	12
+	6	+	1	+	8	+
9	+	3	+	7	+	6
+	2	+	1	+	18	+
13	+	6	+	2	+	7
+	5	+	8	+	3	+
1	+	12	+	16	+	5

Math Path

114

Pick the best starting number, and then go up/down or left/right until you have touched all of the spaces once. What is the *highest* total you can end with? Draw your path.

3	–	1
–	1	–
2	+	4

Total: _____

Sudoku

115

Each row, column, and 2 x 2 box has the digits 1, 2, 3, and 4. Fill in the blanks to complete the puzzle.

4	2	1	3
1			2
3			1
2	1	3	4

In Addition

116

Fill in the blanks with the digits 1–9 so that the sum of each row is the number to the right, and the sum of each column is the number below it.

	7	2	13
6	5		12
			15

16	14	10

117 Thinking of a Number

I'm thinking of a four-digit number in which:

- the first digit is the sum of the other three digits.
- the second, third, and fourth digits are each two apart.
- the fourth digit is bigger than the second.

		3	

118 Fill in the Blanks

Fill in the blanks to make this equation true.

$$
\begin{array}{r}
4\ 3\ \square \\
+\ \ \ \ 6\ 7 \\
\hline
\square\ \square\ 6
\end{array}
$$

119 Math Path

Pick the best starting number, and then go up/down or left/right until you have touched all of the spaces once. What is the *highest* total you can end with? Draw your path.

6	–	4
+	5	–
1	–	2

Total: _____

Addition Challenge

120

Directions:

1. Pick a colored pen. Have your partner pick a different color.

2. One player is on the left, and one player is on the right.

3. Look at the numbers in the middle. In each row, circle the numbers on your side that add up to the number in the middle. You can circle as many numbers as you need. For example:

1	2	3	4	5	(6)	7	(8)	(9)	**23**	9	8	7	6	5	4	3	2	1

4. Once you have circled any combination of numbers, put an **X** on the number in the middle. That row is now closed. You get a point for each **X**.

5. Start at the same time, and solve as many rows as you can before your partner.

6. You do not have to solve the rows in order. (You can start at the end or skip around.)

7. At the end, the person with the most points wins.

Player #1												Player #2									
1	2	3	4	5	6	7	8	9	11	13	**36**	13	11	9	8	7	6	5	4	3	2	1
1	2	3	4	5	6	7	8	9	11	13	**27**	13	11	9	8	7	6	5	4	3	2	1
1	2	3	4	5	6	7	8	9	11	13	**41**	13	11	9	8	7	6	5	4	3	2	1
1	2	3	4	5	6	7	8	9	11	13	**19**	13	11	9	8	7	6	5	4	3	2	1
1	2	3	4	5	6	7	8	9	11	13	**57**	13	11	9	8	7	6	5	4	3	2	1
1	2	3	4	5	6	7	8	9	11	13	**33**	13	11	9	8	7	6	5	4	3	2	1
1	2	3	4	5	6	7	8	9	11	13	**42**	13	11	9	8	7	6	5	4	3	2	1
1	2	3	4	5	6	7	8	9	11	13	**53**	13	11	9	8	7	6	5	4	3	2	1
1	2	3	4	5	6	7	8	9	11	13	**12**	13	11	9	8	7	6	5	4	3	2	1
1	2	3	4	5	6	7	8	9	11	13	**39**	13	11	9	8	7	6	5	4	3	2	1
1	2	3	4	5	6	7	8	9	11	13	**28**	13	11	9	8	7	6	5	4	3	2	1

Sudoku
121

Each row, column, and 2 x 2 box has the digits 1, 2, 3, and 4. Fill in the blanks to complete the puzzle.

3		2	1
2		3	4
1	3		2
4	2		3

In Addition
122

Fill in the blanks with the digits 1–9 so that the sum of each row is the number to the right, and the sum of each column is the number below it.

	6	7		24
9			5	25
	6	5	2	18
4	5	6		16
21	19	27	16	

Thinking of a Number
123

I'm thinking of a four-digit number in which:

- you can get the fourth digit by adding together two of the others.
- the third digit is twice the first.
- the product of the first and second digits is twenty.
- the second digit is larger than the first.

			9

Sudoku

124

Each row, column, and 2 x 2 box has the digits 1, 2, 3, and 4. Fill in the blanks to complete the puzzle.

4		1	
1	2		3
		3	1
	1		4

It's Touching

125

Fill in the blank boxes with the numbers 1–5. Each full row and column contains the numbers 1, 2, 3, 4, and 5. Each shaded number is the sum of all the numbers touching it.

	3	2	1	
	25		25	5
1		3	4	2
3	24	1	22	
4		5	3	

Plus or Minus Game

126

Directions:

1. Find a partner. Each of you will need a copy of this sheet and a different-colored pen.
2. Look at the rows below. In each row, you have to add and/or subtract to get from the first number to the last. The first one has been done for you.
3. Race your partner to solve the rows. You do not have to go in order. The person who solves the most rows wins.
4. Ready, set, go!

| 16 | (+) or − | 3 | + or (−) | 9 | (+) or − | 5 | = | 15 |

| 21 | + or − | 9 | + or − | 4 | + or − | 6 | = | 14 |

| 35 | + or − | 8 | + or − | 7 | + or − | 23 | = | 27 |

| 8 | + or − | 7 | + or − | 17 | + or − | 18 | = | 36 |

| 72 | + or − | 36 | + or − | 18 | + or − | 9 | = | 9 |

| 18 | + or − | 7 | + or − | 9 | + or − | 6 | = | 26 |

| 62 | + or − | 15 | + or − | 6 | + or − | 33 | = | 20 |

| 53 | + or − | 18 | + or − | 4 | + or − | 18 | = | 21 |

Fill in the Blanks

127

Fill in the blanks to make this equation true.

```
    4  5  ☐
 +  3  ☐  3
 _____
    ☐  3  5
```

Math Path

128

Pick the best starting number, and then go up/down or left/right until you have touched all of the spaces once. What is the *highest* total you can end with? Draw your path.

1	–	1
–	4	+
1	+	1

Total: _____

In Addition

129

Fill in the blanks with the digits 1–9 so that the sum of each row is the number to the right, and the sum of each column is the number below it.

8		2		20
3	9		4	21
	6	7	2	20
	5			16

20	23	19	15

Thinking of a Number

130

I'm thinking of a five-digit number in which:

- each digit is the sum of the two digits before it.

1				8

Sudoku

131

Each row, column, and 2 x 2 box has the digits 1, 2, 3, and 4. Fill in the blanks to complete the puzzle.

	3	4	
	1	2	
	2	3	
	4	1	

Operation Box

132

Fill in each blank box with a number so that everything that touches is true and positive.

	=		■
■	13	■	6	■
	−	■	=	
=	■	■	■	−
5	+		=	9

Meet Your Match

133

Directions:

1. Find a partner. Each of you will need a copy of this sheet and a different-colored pen.

2. Look at the left and right sides in the columns below. On each side, there are equations that have the same answer.

3. Draw lines between equations that have the same answer. The first one has been done for you.

4. The person who can draw the most lines wins.

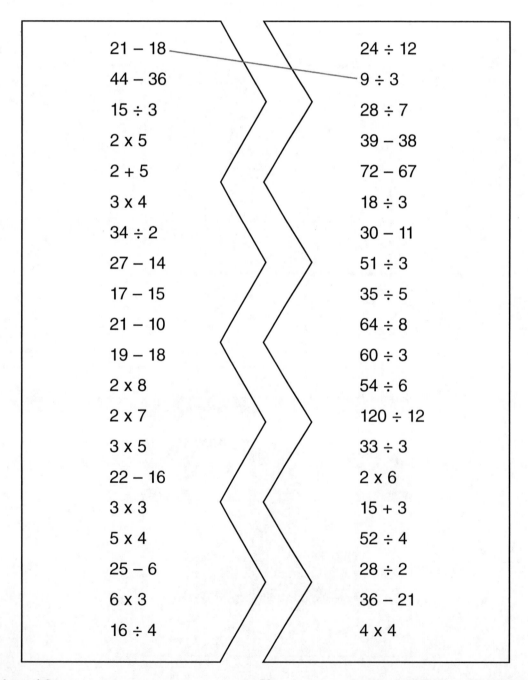

Fill in the Blanks

134

Fill in the blanks to make this equation true.

$$
\begin{array}{r}
3\ \square\ 6\\
+\ \square\ 2\ \square\\
\hline
7\ 9\ 3
\end{array}
$$

Sudoku

135

Each row, column, and 2 x 2 box has the digits 1, 2, 3, and 4. Fill in the blanks to complete the puzzle.

2		1	4
	4		
		3	
3	1		2

It's Touching

136

Fill in the blank boxes with the numbers 1–5. Each full row and column contains the numbers 1, 2, 3, 4, and 5. Each shaded number is the sum of all the numbers touching it.

4	2		5	3
3	22		24	5
	2		1	
1	25		24	2
2	3		4	1

Thinking of a Number

137

I'm thinking of a four-digit number in which:
- each digit is bigger than the one before it.
- the sum of all the digits is thirty.

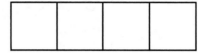

Operation Box

138

Fill in each blank box with a number so that everything that touches is true and positive.

	+	4	■	5
=	■	=	■	=
6	■	8	■	1
−	■	−	■	−
	■		=	

In Addition

139

Fill in the blanks with the digits 1–9 so that the sum of each row is the number to the right, and the sum of each column is the number below it.

			1	**14**
6	3			**17**
3	9	5		**19**
3	1	7		**14**
16	**19**	**17**	**12**	

Tic-Tac-Toe Race

140

Directions:

1. Pick a colored pen. Have your partner pick a different color.
2. Choose a tic-tac-toe board, and sit side by side.
3. Start at the same time, and race to solve the math problems.
4. When you solve a problem, write the answer in the box.
5. If you get three in a row, you win!
6. Check your answers. If your partner wrote a wrong answer, the space is yours!

Example:

$6 - 4$	$4 + 2$	$8 - 3$
$9 + 5$ 14	$4 + 5$	$2 + 7$
$1 + 6$	$3 + 9$	$7 - 5$

Game Boards:

$36 \div 3$	9×7	$134 - 47$
$121 \div 11$	17×13	14×6
$125 \div 5$	12×21	$247 - 168$

$192 - 98$	24×9	$347 + 586$
$68 \div 4$	116×8	$216 \div 36$
95×7	$657 - 378$	33×13

$729 - 555$	$368 + 572$	26×14
13×18	$364 \div 14$	$72 \div 6$
23×24	$444 + 555$	$364 \div 26$

23×8	22×5	$366 + 178$
$98 \div 14$	$552 \div 23$	$793 + 8$
$672 + 219$	9×90	19×6

Fill in the Blanks
141

Fill in the blanks to make this equation true.

$$
\begin{array}{r}
3\ \square\ \square \\
+\ 1\ 6\ 7 \\
\hline
\square\ 4\ 9
\end{array}
$$

Math Path
142

Pick the best starting number, and then go up/down or left/right until you have touched all of the spaces once. What is the *highest* total you can end with? Draw your path.

2	–	1
–	1	–
1	+	3

Total: _____

Sudoku
143

Each row, column, and 2 x 3 box has the digits 1, 2, 3, 4, 5, and 6. Fill in the blanks to complete the puzzle.

2	1	4			
5	3	6		2	4
		1	3		2
3		2	5		
	2		4	6	5
	6		2		1

Thinking of a Number

144

I'm thinking of a four-digit number in which:
- the sum of the third and fourth digits is fifteen.
- the sum of the first and second digits is fifteen.
- the sum of the second and third digits is fourteen.
- the fourth digit is larger than the first.

In Addition

145

Fill in the blanks with the digits 1–9 so that the sum of each row is the number to the right, and the sum of each column is the number below it.

		8	4	17
9		2		23
7		2	8	18
6			2	16

25	13	17	19

It's Touching

146

Fill in the blank boxes with the numbers 1–5. Each full row and column contains the numbers 1, 2, 3, 4, and 5. Each shaded number is the sum of all the numbers touching it.

	3	1	4	
3	23		23	4
5		2	1	3
4	28	5	23	1
	3	4	5	

Snake Race

147

Directions:

1. Find a partner. Each player should use a different-colored pen.

2. Sit side by side, and put the game board in front of you.

3. Look for snakes that equal twenty-four. The numbers have to be touching. (You cannot jump around.)

4. You may use a number more than once.

5. Take turns. You have 30 seconds to find a snake.

6. If you cannot find a snake in 30 seconds, the other person wins.

Example:

8	+	4	+
+	9	+	12
7	+	6	+
+	8	+	3

Game Board:

50	÷	2	–	1	+	3	x	6
–	31	x	2	–	23	+	3	+
25	+	12	+	17	–	8	+	15
–	5	+	1	x	4	+	4	x
1	+	7	+	5	+	8	x	3
+	4	x	6	+	3	–	1	+
15	+	3	+	16	+	8	–	17
+	5	+	4	–	2	x	12	+
8	x	3	x	8	x	1	–	4

Fill in the Blanks

148

Fill in the blanks to make this equation true.

$$
\begin{array}{r}
5\ \square\ \square \\
+\ \square\ 2\ 6 \\
\hline
8\ 3\ 3
\end{array}
$$

Sudoku

149

Each row, column, and 2 x 3 box has the digits 1, 2, 3, 4, 5, and 6. Fill in the blanks to complete the puzzle.

	6		3	4	5
5		3		1	6
		4	1	3	2
	3	2	6		
4	1			2	
	2	5	4	6	

Math Path

150

Pick the best starting number, and then go up/down or left/right until you have touched all of the spaces once. What is the *highest* total you can end with? Draw your path.

9	–	5
–	3	–
1	+	3

Total: _____

151 Operation Box

Fill in each blank box with a number so that everything that touches is true and positive.

7	=	4	−	
=	■	■	■	=
	+	3	■	
■	■	■	■	+
	−	14	=	3

152 In Addition

Fill in the blanks with the digits 1–9 so that the sum of each row is the number to the right, and the sum of each column is the number below it.

2				21
	5	6	5	19
5	9	2		23
		1	4	12

15	23	13	24

Sudoku

153

Each row, column, and 2 x 3 box has the digits 1, 2, 3, 4, 5, and 6. Fill in the blanks to complete the puzzle.

	2	1	6		
6	4		5	1	
		2	1	3	6
1	3		4		5
	1	5		6	4
3		4	2		

It's Touching

154

Fill in the blank boxes with the numbers 1–5. Each full row and column contains the numbers 1, 2, 3, 4, and 5. Each shaded number is the sum of all the numbers touching it.

4	1	5	3	
1	26	3	24	
5	25	2	22	
2	3	1	4	

155 Miguel, Anna, Tran, and Lisa

Miguel, Anna, Tran, and Lisa went on vacation, each to a different place. Read each clue. Then, mark the chart to see who went where.

Clues:

✔ Miguel went somewhere in the United States.

✔ Tran went to Florida.

✔ Lisa didn't go to Italy.

Travel Diary

	Hawaii	Mexico	Italy	Florida
Miguel				
Anna				
Tran				
Lisa				

Answers:

Where did Miguel go?

_____

Where did Anna go?

_____

Where did Tran go?

_____

Where did Lisa go?

_____

156 How Old?

Brian is five years younger than his older brother.

In two years, his brother will be twice as old as Brian is now.

How old are Brian and his brother?

_____

_____

Logic Puzzles

Four-in-a-Row

Directions:

1. Find a partner.

2. Choose **X**s or **O**s.

3. Take turns putting an **X** or an **O** in a box.

4. Try to make four in a row, either up-and-down or right-and-left (no diagonals).

5. At the end, count how many four-in-a-rows you made. The person who makes the most wins.

6. If you have time, play again!

Example:

X	X	X	X	O	O
O	O	X	X	O	O
X	X	X	X	O	O
X	X	X	X	O	X
O	O	O	O	X	O
O	O	X	O	O	X

Game Boards:

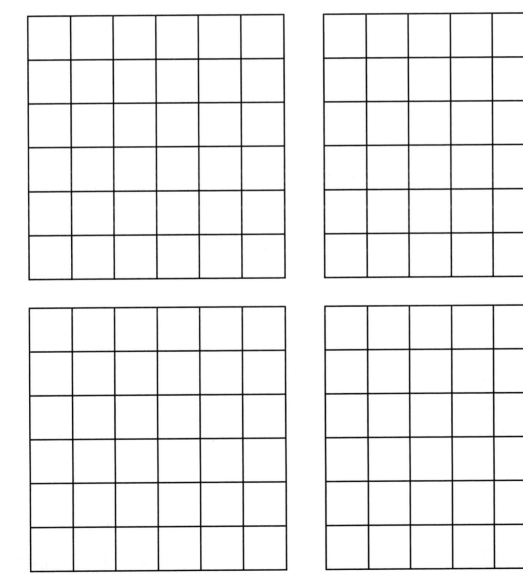

What's Next?

158

Draw the shape that should come next.

$$\bigcirc \bigcirc \square \square \bigcirc \bigcirc \triangle \triangle \bigcirc \bigcirc \square \square \bigcirc \bigcirc \triangle \triangle \_\_\_$$

Adam's Coat

159

Adam lost his coat. Can you help him find it? Circle the correct coat.

Here are facts about Adam's coat:

✔ It does not have a zipper.

✔ It has three buttons.

✔ It has two pockets.

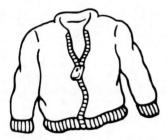  

Miguel, Anna, Tran, and Lisa

160

Miguel, Anna, Tran, and Lisa want to have different careers when they grow up. Read each clue. Then, mark the chart to see who wants which career.

Clues:

✔ Tran wants to be either a teacher or the President.

✔ Neither Miguel nor Anna wants to be a doctor.

✔ Miguel doesn't want to be a lawyer or the President.

	President	Doctor	Lawyer	Teacher
Miguel				
Anna				
Tran				
Lisa				

Answers:

What does Miguel want to be?

_____

What does Anna want to be?

_____

What does Tran want to be?

_____

What does Lisa want to be?

_____

Odd Animal Out

161

Circle the animal that doesn't belong.

   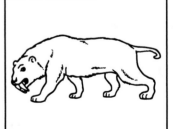

Why doesn't it belong? _____

Add One or Two

162

Directions:

1. Find a partner. Each player should use a different-colored pen.
2. Look at the boxes below.
3. Take turns coloring in boxes.
4. You can color in either one or two boxes per turn.
5. Whoever colors in the last box wins.
6. If you have time, play again. This time whoever colors in the last box loses!

Example:

Game Boards:

1.

2.

3.

4.

5.

6.

Jim's Jump Rope

Jim lost his jump rope. Can you help him find it? Circle the correct jump rope.

Here are facts about Jim's jump rope:

✔ It doesn't have handles.

✔ It has black stripes.

✔ It is long.

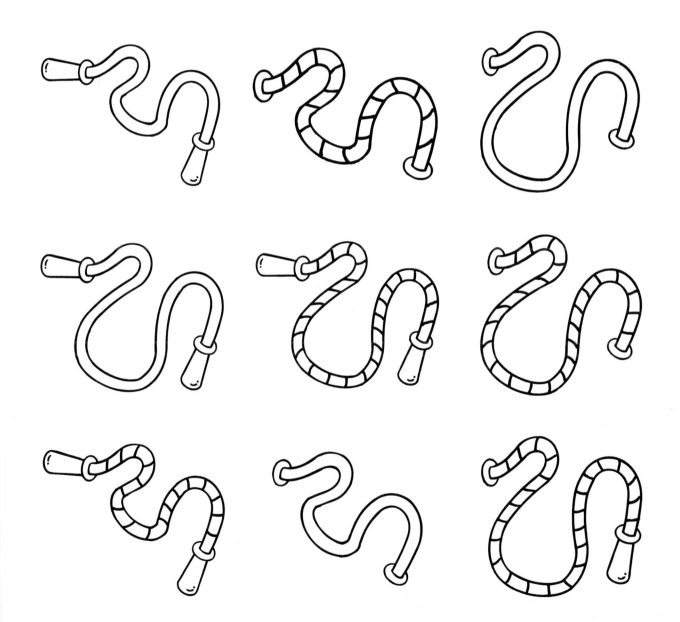

164 What's Next?

Draw the shape that should come next.

○□○△○□○△○△○□○△△○□○△△△○□○___

165 How Old?

Mei and her sister are identical twins.

The sum of their ages is twenty-two.

How old are Mei and her sister?

_____

_____

166 Letter Box

Put the letters A, B, C, and D in the boxes so that:

- D is directly left of A and directly above C.

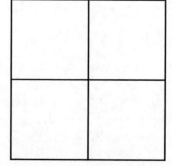

Reversi

167

Directions:

1. Find a partner and two pencils.

2. One of you is **X**s and the other is **O**s.

3. Take turns marking your letter (**X** or **O**) on the game board.

4. Try to trap your partner's letter between two of yours. If you trap a letter, it turns into yours—erase the trapped letter and replace it with your own.

5. At the end, the person with the most letters on the board wins!

Example:

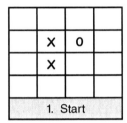
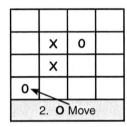
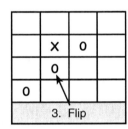
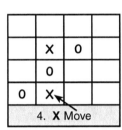
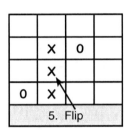

Game Board:

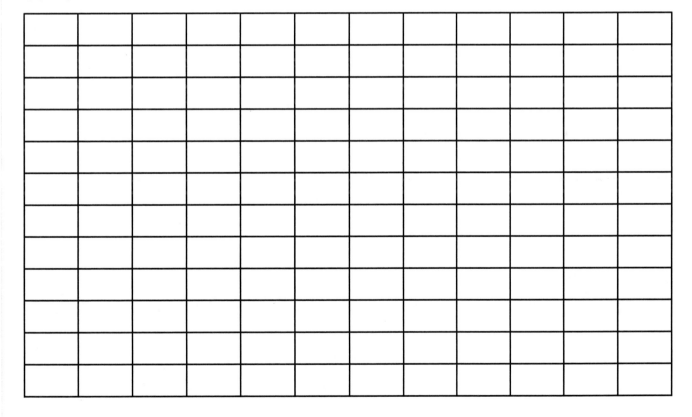

Miguel, Anna, Tran, and Lisa

168

Miguel, Anna, Tran, and Lisa each like a different school subject. Read each clue. Then, mark the chart to see who prefers which subject.

Clues:

✔ Anna's favorite is not music or science.

✔ Miguel's favorite is not music or reading.

✔ Lisa's favorite is not music, science, or reading.

	Math	Reading	Music	Science
Miguel				
Anna				
Tran				
Lisa				

Answers:

What is Miguel's favorite subject?

_____

What is Anna's favorite subject?

_____

What is Tran's favorite subject?

_____

What is Lisa's favorite subject?

_____

Letter Box

169

Put the letters A, B, C, and D in the boxes so that:

• B and A are in the bottom row.

• D and A are in the left column.

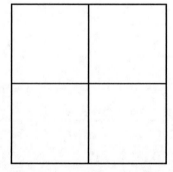

Corinne's Necklace

170

Corinne lost her necklace. Can you help her find it? Circle the correct necklace.

Here are facts about Corinne's necklace:

✔   It has a small heart pendant.

✔   It does not have a clasp.

✔   It does not have beads.

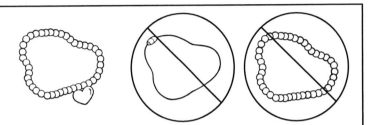

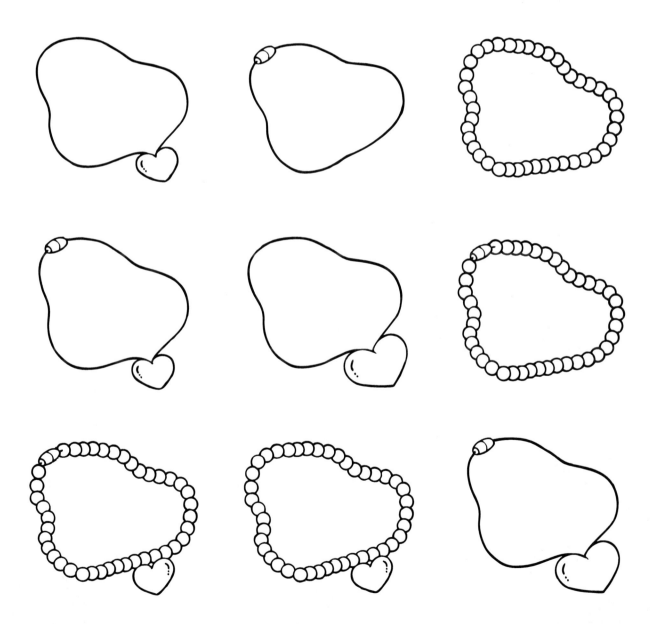

Blocked

Directions:

1. Find a partner and two pencils.

2. Take turns drawing lines from one dot to another. You can draw only vertical lines, and your partner can draw only horizontal lines.

3. Once any line touches a dot, the dot is closed and cannot be used again.

4. The first person who cannot make a move loses.

5. If you have time, make your own board and play again.

Example:

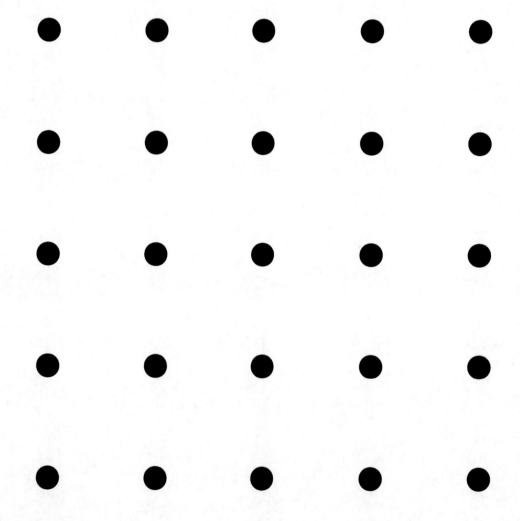

Game Board:

What's Next?

172

Draw the shape that should come next.

$$\bigcirc\bigcirc\triangle\bigcirc\bigcirc\bigcirc\square\square\bigcirc\bigcirc\triangle\bigcirc\bigcirc\bigcirc\square\square\bigcirc\bigcirc\_\_\_$$

How Old?

173

Right now, Riley is three times as old as her sister.

The sum of their ages is twelve.

How old are Riley and her sister?

_____

_____

Odd Animal Out

174

Circle the animal that doesn't belong.

Why doesn't it belong? _____

Letter Box

175

Put the letters B, C, and D in the boxes so that:

- A and B are not in the same row or column.
- B and D are in the same row.

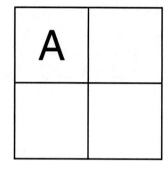

Miguel, Anna, Tran, and Lisa

176

Miguel, Anna, Tran, and Lisa each like a different kind of music. Read each clue. Then, mark the chart to see who prefers which kind of music.

Clues:

✔ Tran can't stand hip-hop or rock.

✔ Neither Anna nor Lisa likes classical music or hip-hop.

✔ Anna loves jazz.

	Jazz	Hip-Hop	Rock	Classical
Miguel				
Anna				
Tran				
Lisa				

Answers:

What is Miguel's favorite kind of music?

_____

What is Anna's favorite kind of music?

_____

What is Tran's favorite kind of music?

_____

What is Lisa's favorite kind of music?

_____

Boxed Out

Directions:

1. Find a partner. Each player should use a different-colored pen.

2. Look at the dots below.

3. Take turns drawing a short line between two dots.

4. Try to make closed boxes. When you make a box, color it in. Then, go again.

5. The person who makes the most boxes wins.

Example:

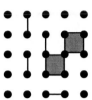

Game Board:

Katy's Binder

Katy lost her school binder. Can you help her find it? Circle the correct binder.

Here are facts about Katy's binder:

✔ It has stripes and Katy's name on the front.

✔ It is square.

✔ It does not have stars on it.

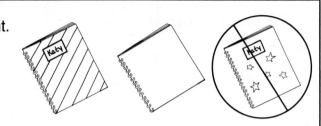

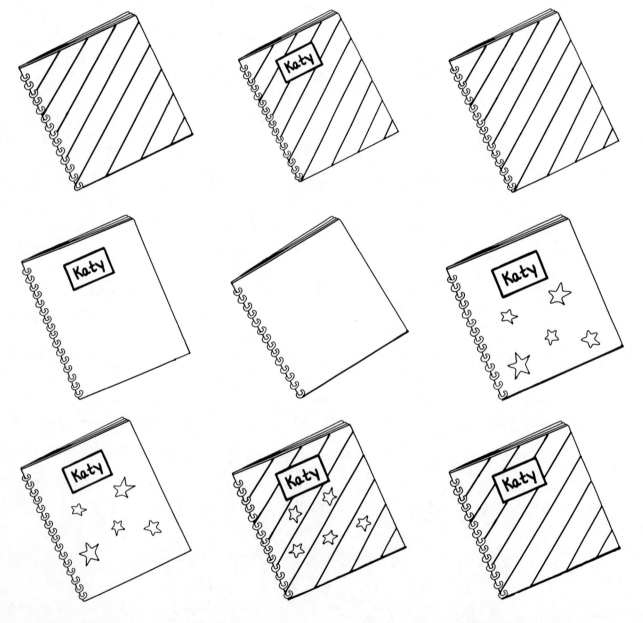

How Old?
179

In five years, Seth will be three times as old as his brother is right now.

In five years, his brother will be nine.

How old are Seth and his brother right now?

_____

_____

Letter Box
180

Put the letters A, B, C, and D in the boxes so that:

- moving clockwise, the letters read A, D, C, B.
- D is directly left of C.

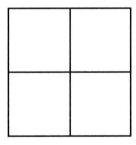

Odd Animal Out
181

Circle the animal that doesn't belong.

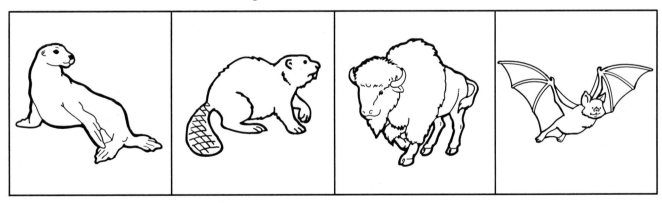

Why doesn't it belong? _____

Ship Shapes

Directions:

1. Find a partner. You will each need two copies of the game board below.
2. On one of your game boards, color in the following "ships." You can mark them up-and-down or left-and-right (vertically or horizontally). Don't show your partner!

Aircraft Carrier: Battleship: Cruiser:

Patrol Boat: Submarine:

3. Take turns trying to find each other's ships. For example, you might say "A8" and your partner would say "hit" or "miss." Mark your guesses on your blank game board. Mark your partner's guesses on the game board with your ships. Hide your game boards while you are playing!
4. Once your partner has hit every space of one of your ships, it is sunk.
5. The first person to sink all of the other's ships wins.

Game Board:

	1	2	3	4	5	6	7	8	9	10
A										
B										
C										
D										
E										
F										
G										
H										
I										
J										

Logic Puzzles

183 What's Next?

Draw the shape that should come next.

◯◯▢◯◯△△◯◯◯▢◯◯◯△△◯◯ ____

184 Miguel, Anna, Tran, and Lisa

Miguel, Anna, Tran, and Lisa each play a different position on their baseball team. Read each clue. Then, mark the chart to see who plays which position.

Clues:

✔ Lisa doesn't play pitcher or catcher.

✔ A boy plays first base.

✔ A girl plays pitcher.

✔ Miguel doesn't play catcher.

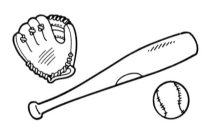

	Outfield	Pitcher	Catcher	First Base
Miguel				
Anna				
Tran				
Lisa				

Answers:

Which position does Miguel play?

_____

Which position does Anna play?

_____

Which position does Tran play?

_____

Which position does Lisa play?

_____

Liza's Magic Wand

Liza's magic wand has disappeared! Can you help her find it? Circle the correct magic wand.

Here are facts about Liza's magic wand:

✔   It has a star on the end of it.

✔   It does not have stripes.

✔   It is long.

How Old?

186

Sometime in the past, the sum of Matt's age and his sister's age was nineteen.

Matt was born in 1995, and his sister was born in 1998.

What year was it when the sum of their ages was nineteen?

_____

Letter Box

187

Put the letters A, B, C, and D in the boxes so that:

- A is diagonally up and right from D.
- C is not in the bottom row.

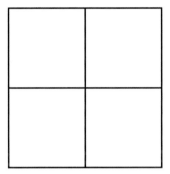

Odd Animal Out

188

Circle the animal that doesn't belong.

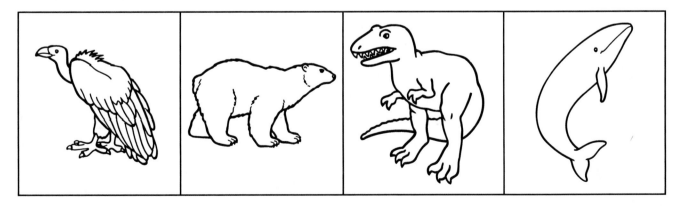

Why doesn't it belong? _____

What's Next?

189

Draw the shape that should come next.

Miguel, Anna, Tran, and Lisa

190

Miguel, Anna, Tran, and Lisa each have a different favorite dessert. Read each clue. Then, mark the chart to see who prefers which dessert.

Clues:

✔ Lisa's favorite dessert is not cake.

✔ Tran's favorite dessert is not candy or cookies.

✔ A boy chose cookies as his favorite dessert.

✔ A girl chose cake as her favorite dessert.

	Ice Cream	Candy	Cookies	Cake
Miguel				
Anna				
Tran				
Lisa				

Answers:

What is Miguel's favorite dessert?

_____

What is Anna's favorite dessert?

_____

What is Tran's favorite dessert?

_____

What is Lisa's favorite dessert?

_____

Answer Key

Note: Answers are organized according to puzzle number, not page number.

Picture Puzzles

1. ten

2.

3. The giraffe with one hump is not a real animal.

4. knock on wood
   crossroads

5. In the second picture, the banana has a bite taken out of it. The monkey has a ring on its finger and no tail. The monkey also has its eyes closed and is licking its lips.

7.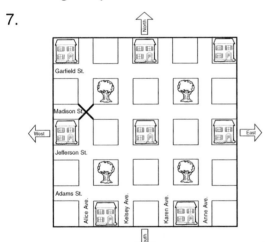

8.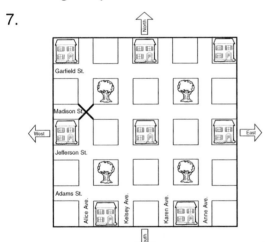

9. In the second picture, there is no fire coming out the back end, the tip of the shuttle is white, the left wing is missing, the cargo doors are missing, and Earth is gone.

11.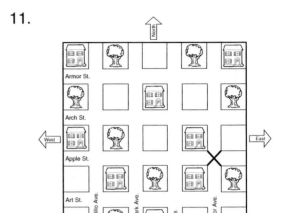

12. The lion with horns is not a real animal.

13. In the second picture, the boy is wearing a striped shirt and a cap with a black brim. He has taken a bite of his sandwich. In addition, his dog has spots, and the pitcher is missing from the table.

15.

16. fourteen (*Note:* The large box is a square.)

17. 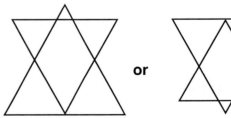 **or**

18. Read between the lines.
    deep in thought

19. The iguana with buckteeth is not a real animal.

Answer Key *(cont.)*

20.
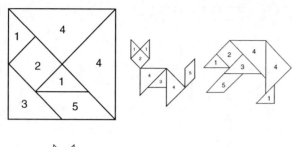

 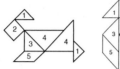

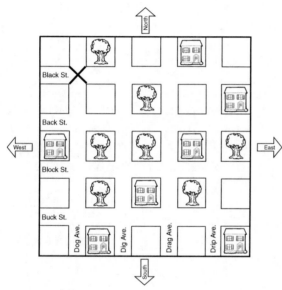

21.
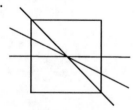

28.
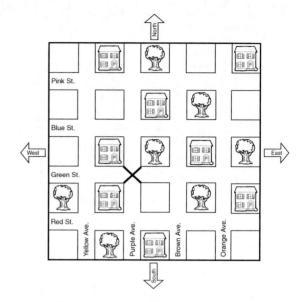

30.
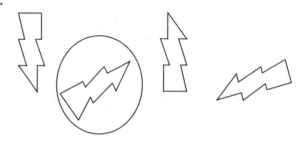

22. twenty-one

23. In the second picture, the boy is wearing knee pads and has no socks on. He is missing his chin strap and left glove. Also, his skateboard is missing one wheel.

25.
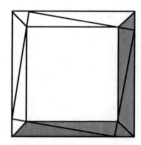

26. jack-in-the-box
    long underwear

27. The seagull with a dragon's tail is not a real animal.

31. thirteen

32. I understand.
    square meal

33.

34. The spider with six legs is not a real animal.

35. In the second picture, the web is missing strands, the spider is missing two legs, there is a fly stuck in the web, the spider has fangs, and the spider no longer has dots on its face.

Answer Key *(cont.)*

37.

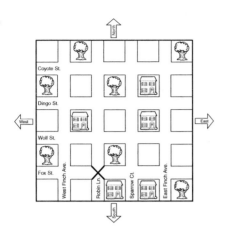

38.

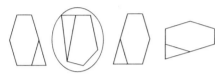

39. nineteen

Word Puzzles

40. pen, jump, ump and pump, plum, plump, and lump, open, plan, impossible

41. Answers will vary but may be similar to:

b	r	a	g
b	**r**	**a**	**t**
b	**e**	**a**	**t**
n	e	a	t

42.

¹ c	² a	³ r	⁴ e
⁵ o	p	e	n
⁶ r	e	a	d
⁷ e	r	r	s

43. The bowl's crunchy enamel was enough to anger Bill.

44. a coconut

45. mango, papaya, apricot, banana

46.

		B	E	A	R			
		I						
Z	E	B	R	A				
		D						
		L	I	Z	A	R	D	
		E				E		
						E		
			H	O	R	S	E	

Other words will vary.

47. rats, star, arts
Sentences will vary.

48. Common keywords to realize Brazil are rainfall, Amazon, and soccer.

49.

¹ s	² t	³ i	⁴ r
⁵ h	i	d	e
⁶ o	p	e	n
⁷ p	s	s	t

50. a watchdog

51. Answers will vary but may be similar to:

d	o	g	s
d	**o**	**e**	**s**
t	**o**	**e**	**s**
t	o	y	s

52. stew, wets, west
Sentences will vary.

54. The okapi ran hard and tried to grab bits of food.

55. tomato, spinach, potato, cucumber

56.

¹ m	² i	³ l	⁴ k
⁵ i	r	o	n
⁶ n	i	l	e
⁷ i	s	l	e

Answer Key *(cont.)*

57. Answers will vary but may be similar to:

s	l	e	d
s	**e**	**e**	**d**
s	**e**	**n**	**d**
b	e	n	d

58. cookie, apple pie, fudge, sundae

59. your name

60. Answers will vary but may include: beginning, winning, well, wain, went, spinning, spell, Spain, spent, space, agency, again, agent, ancient, palace, emergency, emergent, brain, brace, efficiency, efficient

61.

¹s	²e	³e	⁴n
⁵p	a	c	e
⁶a	c	h	e
⁷s	h	o	d

62. My grand(mother) (feels) you should always capital(ize) Brandon.

63. pits, spit, tips
    Sentences will vary.

64. sun, suspense, mississippi, splash, shoe, hose and hoes, slip, lisp, and lips

65. violet, carnation, poppy, sunflower

66. the bat boy

67. Order may vary.

    car → rat → train →

    ninja → arm → magnet →

    tuba → airplane → elephant

68. The s(cowl)ing wizard(s' wa)nds made the li(mo) useless.

69. CAT

70.

¹t	²h	³a	⁴t
⁵h	a	r	e
⁶e	v	e	n
⁷n	e	a	t

71. a lighthouse

72. bared, beard, bread
    Sentences will vary.

73. prairie, valley, river, ocean

74. potato, otter, twitch and witch, trap and rapt, hat and that, star and start

76. Answers will vary but may be similar to:

m	i	s	t
m	**o**	**s**	**t**
h	**o**	**s**	**t**
h	o	s	e

77. DOG

78. plan, seat, mast, aardvark, ape and pea, are and area, sap, asp, and spa

79.

¹s	²h	³i	⁴p
⁵h	i	d	e
⁶a	r	e	a
⁷d	e	a	r

80. FOX

81. chess, tic-tac-toe, checkers, bingo

82.

				B			
				R			
		C	E	R	E	A	L
	C		A				
S	A	N	D	W	I	C	H
	T					A	
	N					K	
	I	C	E	C	R	E	A	M
	P						

Others words will vary.

83. Answers will vary but may be similar to:

p	a	c	k
p	**i**	**c**	**k**
l	**i**	**c**	**k**
l	i	c	e

Answer Key *(cont.)*

84. The (flea) gleefully (came) (late) to the b(l)ob's te(a)m party.

85.

¹ b	² e	³ s	⁴ t
⁵ o	l	e	o
⁶ a	s	a	p
⁷ s	e	t	s

86. ace, crouch, cat and act, speech, cracker, chitchat

87. FISH

88. Answers will vary but may be similar to:

o	p	e	n
o	**v**	**e**	**n**
o	**v**	**e**	**r**
e	v	e	r

90. rang, globe, gore and ogre, gurgle, girl, juggle

91. an umbrella

92. grocery, hardware, pharmacy,W department

93. WORM

94. I'll have the propo(sal Mon)day for the uni(ver)sal mo(ney).

95.

¹ s	² h	³ u	⁴ t
⁵ h	o	s	e
⁶ o	p	e	n
⁷ t	e	s	t

97. A shadow

98. mixer, blender, toaster, waffle iron

99.

¹ p	² e	³ s	⁴ t
⁵ o	v	e	r
⁶ d	e	m	o
⁷ s	n	i	t

100. PIGEON

101. Answers will vary but may be similar to:

m	o	o	n
m	**o**	**o**	**d**
m	**o**	**l**	**d**
c	o	l	d

102.

¹ a	² b	³ l	⁴ e
⁵ l	o	a	n
⁶ s	l	i	d
⁷ o	a	r	s

Number Puzzles

103.

3	1	8	12
4	2	9	15
8	4	7	19

15	7	24

104. 10

Paths will vary but may be similar to:

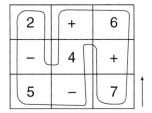

Answer Key *(cont.)*

105.

2	3	4	**1**
4	**1**	2	3
1	2	**3**	4
3	4	1	2

106.

5	2	5	6	18
4	6	**9**	6	25
2	**4**	**2**	**5**	13
1	**6**	7	2	16

12	18	23	19

107.

6 x 4	8 x 9	32 – 17		48 + 34	75 – 27	3 x 9
24	72	15		82	48	27
54 + 31	47 – 39	5 x 8		3 + 2	4 x 9	33 + 29
85	8	40		5	36	62
86 – 38	7 x 6	23 + 48		9 x 5	35 + 73	52 – 33
48	42	71		45	108	19

64 – 45	7 x 7	16 + 62		34 – 17	4 x 7	47 – 34
19	49	78		17	28	13
8 x 9	98 – 89	39 + 49		5 x 5	7 x 3	45 – 44
72	9	88		25	21	1
12 + 89	8 x 6	37 – 18		6 x 9	54 + 47	33 + 29
101	48	19		54	101	62

108. 9

Paths will vary but may be similar to:

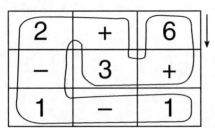

109.

2	**3**	**6**	**9**

110.

■	■		=	**6**
=	**3**	+	**3**	■
6	■	3	■	7
–	■		**5**	=
4	=	**2**	+	■

111.

1	**3**	**4**	2
4	2	1	3
2	1	3	4
3	**4**	**2**	1

112.

4	**9**	4	17
5	6	7	18
3	**1**	8	12

12	16	19

113. Answers will vary but may be similar to:

14	+	3	+	1	+	12
+	6	+	1	+	8	+
9	+	3	+	7	+	6
+	2	+	1	+	18	+
13	+	6	+	2	+	7
+	5	+	8	+	3	+
1	+	12	+	16	+	5

114. 3

Paths will vary but may be similar to:

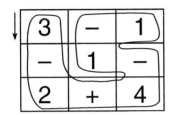

115.

4	2	1	3
1	3	4	2
3	4	2	1
2	1	3	4

116.

4	7	2	13
6	5	1	12
6	2	7	15

16	14	10

117.

9	1	3	5

118.

```
    4  3  9
 +     6  7
 ─────────────
    5  0  6
```

119. 4

Paths will vary but may be similar to:

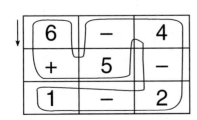

120. Answers will vary but may be similar to:

Player #1											Sum	Player #2										
1	2	3	4	5	6	7	8	9	11	13	36	13	11	9	8	7	6	5	4	3	2	1
1	2	3	4	5	6	7	8	9	11	13	27	13	11	9	8	7	6	5	4	3	2	1
1	2	3	4	5	6	7	8	9	11	13	41	13	11	9	8	7	6	5	4	3	2	1
1	2	3	4	5	6	7	8	9	11	13	19	13	11	9	8	7	6	5	4	3	2	1
1	2	3	4	5	6	7	8	9	11	13	57	13	11	9	8	7	6	5	4	3	2	1
1	2	3	4	5	6	7	8	9	11	13	33	13	11	9	8	7	6	5	4	3	2	1
1	2	3	4	5	6	7	8	9	11	13	42	13	11	9	8	7	6	5	4	3	2	1
1	2	3	4	5	6	7	8	9	11	13	53	13	11	9	8	7	6	5	4	3	2	1
1	2	3	4	5	6	7	8	9	11	13	12	13	11	9	8	7	6	5	4	3	2	1
1	2	3	4	5	6	7	8	9	11	13	39	13	11	9	8	7	6	5	4	3	2	1
1	2	3	4	5	6	7	8	9	11	13	28	13	11	9	8	7	6	5	4	3	2	1

121.

3	4	2	1
2	1	3	4
1	3	4	2
4	2	1	3

122.

3	6	7	8	24
9	2	9	5	25
5	6	5	2	18
4	5	6	1	16

21	19	27	16

123.

4	5	8	9

Answer Key (cont.)

124.

4	3	1	2
1	2	4	3
2	4	3	1
3	1	2	4

125.

5	3	2	1	4
2	25	4	25	5
1	5	3	4	2
3	24	1	22	3
4	2	5	3	1

126.

16	(+) or −	3	+ or (−)	9	(+) or −	5	=	15
21	+ or (−)	9	+ or (−)	4	(+) or −	6	=	14
35	(+) or −	8	(+) or −	7	+ or (−)	23	=	27
8	+ or (−)	7	(+) or −	17	(+) or −	18	=	36
72	+ or (−)	36	+ or (−)	18	+ or (−)	9	=	9
18	+ or (−)	7	(+) or −	9	(+) or −	6	=	26
62	+ or (−)	15	(+) or −	6	+ or (−)	33	=	20
53	+ or (−)	18	(+) or −	4	+ or (−)	18	=	21

127.

```
    4  5  [2]
 +  3  [8] 3
 ─────────────
   [8] 3  5
```

128. 4

Paths will vary but may be similar to:

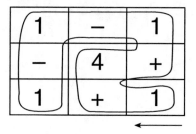

129.

8	3	2	7	20
3	9	5	4	21
5	6	7	2	20
4	5	5	2	16
20	23	19	15	

130.

1	2	3	5	8

131.

2	3	4	1
4	1	2	3
1	2	3	4
3	4	1	2

132.

7	=	7	■
■	13	■	6
8	−	■	=	3
=	■	■	−
5	+	4	=	9

Answer Key *(cont.)*

133.

Left	Right
(3) 21 – 18	24 ÷ 12 (2)
(8) 44 – 36	9 ÷ 3 (3)
(5) 15 ÷ 3	28 ÷ 7 (4)
(10) 2 x 5	39 – 38 (1)
(7) 2 + 5	72 – 67 (5)
(12) 3 x 4	18 ÷ 3 (6)
(17) 34 ÷ 2	30 – 11 (19)
(13) 27 – 14	51 ÷ 3 (17)
(2) 17 – 15	35 ÷ 5 (7)
(11) 21 – 10	64 ÷ 8 (8)
(1) 19 – 18	60 ÷ 3 (20)
(16) 2 x 8	54 ÷ 6 (9)
(14) 2 x 7	120 ÷ 12 (10)
(15) 3 x 5	33 ÷ 3 (11)
(6) 22 – 16	2 x 6 (12)
(9) 3 x 3	15 + 3 (18)
(20) 5 x 4	52 ÷ 4 (13)
(19) 25 – 6	28 ÷ 2 (14)
(18) 6 x 3	36 – 21 (15)
(4) 16 ÷ 4	4 x 4 (16)

134.

```
  3  [6]  6
+[4]  2  [7]
 ─────────
  7   9   3
```

135.

2	3	1	4
1	4	2	3
4	2	3	1
3	1	4	2

136.

4	2	1	5	3
3	22	2	24	5
5	2	3	1	4
1	25	4	24	2
2	3	5	4	1

137.

6	7	8	9

138.

4	+	4	■	5
=	■	=	■	=
6	■	8	■	1
–	■	–	■	–
10	■	2	=	6

139.

4	6	3	1		14
6	3	2	6		17
3	9	5	2		19
3	1	7	3		14

16	19	17	12

140.

36 ÷ 3	9 x 7	134 – 47		192 – 98	24 x 9	347 + 586
12	63	87		94	216	933
121 ÷ 11	17 x 13	14 x 6		68 ÷ 4	116 x 8	216 ÷ 36
11	221	84		17	928	6
125 ÷ 5	12 x 21	247 – 168		95 x 7	657 – 378	33 x 13
25	252	79		665	279	429

729 – 555	368 + 572	26 x 14		23 x 8	22 x 5	366 + 178
174	940	364		184	110	544
13 x 18	364 ÷ 14	72 ÷ 6		98 ÷ 14	552 ÷ 23	793 + 8
234	26	12		7	24	801
23 x 24	444 + 555	364 ÷ 26		672 + 219	9 x 90	19 x 6
552	999	14		891	810	114

141.

```
  3  [8]  [2]
+  1   6   7
 ──────────
 [5]  4   9
```

142. 2

Paths will vary but may be similar to:

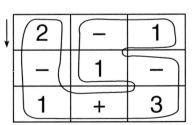

Answer Key *(cont.)*

143.

2	1	4	**6**	**5**	**3**
5	**3**	6	**1**	**2**	4
6	**5**	1	3	**4**	2
3	**4**	2	5	**1**	**6**
1	2	**3**	4	6	5
4	6	**5**	2	**3**	1

144.

7	**8**	**6**	**9**

145.

3	2	8	4	17
9	7	2	5	23
7	1	2	8	18
6	3	5	2	16
25	13	17	19	

146.

2	3	1	4	**5**
3	23	3	23	4
5	4	2	1	3
4	28	5	23	1
1	3	4	5	**2**

147. Answers will vary but may be similar to:

50	÷	2	–	1	+	3	x	6
–	31	x	2	–	23	+	3	+
25	+	12	+	17	–	8	+	15
–	5	+	1	x	4	+	4	x
1	+	7	+	5	+	8	x	3
+	4	x	6	+	3	–	1	+
15	+	3	+	16	+	8	–	17
+	5	+	4	–	2	x	12	+
8	x	3	x	8	x	1	–	4

148.

$$
\begin{array}{r}
5\ \boxed{0}\ \boxed{7} \\
+\ \boxed{3}\ 2\ 6 \\
\hline
8\ \ 3\ \ 3
\end{array}
$$

149.

2	6	**1**	3	4	5
5	**4**	3	**2**	1	6
6	**5**	4	1	3	2
1	3	2	6	**5**	**4**
4	1	**6**	**5**	2	3
3	2	5	4	6	**1**

150. 3

Paths will vary but may be similar to:

9	–	5
–	3	–
1	+	3

151.

7	=	4	–	**11**
=	■			=
4	+	3	■	**8**
■				+
17	–	14	=	3

152.

2	**7**	4	**8**	21
3	5	6	5	19
5	9	2	**7**	23
5	**2**	1	4	12
15	23	13	24	

Answer Key *(cont.)*

153.

5	2	1	6	4	3
6	4	3	5	1	2
4	5	2	1	3	6
1	3	6	4	2	5
2	1	5	3	6	4
3	6	4	2	5	1

154.

4	1	5	3	2
1	26	3	24	4
3	5	4	2	1
5	25	2	22	3
2	3	1	4	5

Logic Puzzles

155.

	Hawaii	Mexico	Italy	Florida
Miguel				
Anna				
Tran				
Lisa				

Where did Miguel go? _____ Hawaii _____

Where did Anna go? _____ Italy _____

Where did Tran go? _____ Florida _____

Where did Lisa go? _____ Mexico _____

156. Brian is seven and his brother is twelve.

158.

159. Adam's coat has three buttons and two pockets.

160.

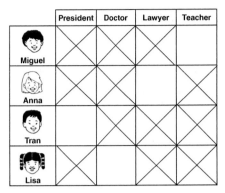

What does Miguel want to be? _____ a teacher _____

What does Anna want to be? _____ a lawyer _____

What does Tran want to be? _____ the President _____

What does Lisa want to be? _____ a doctor _____

161. The camel does not belong because it is the only animal that is not extinct. Or, the T-rex does not belong because it doesn't walk on four legs or have fur.

163. Jim's jump rope is long and has black stripes.

164.

165. Mei and her sister are eleven.

166.

D	A
C	B

168.

	Math	Reading	Music	Science
Miguel				
Anna				
Tran				
Lisa				

What is Miguel's favorite subject? _____ science _____

What is Anna's favorite subject? _____ reading _____

What is Tran's favorite subject? _____ music _____

What is Lisa's favorite subject? _____ math _____

Answer Key *(cont.)*

169.

D	C
A	B

170. Corinne's necklace has a small heart pendant.

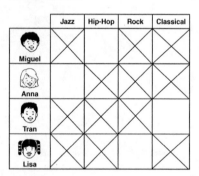

172.

173. Riley is nine and her sister is three.

174. The penguin does not belong because it cannot fly.

175.

A	C
D	B

176.

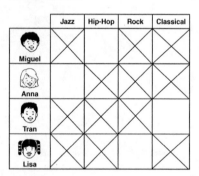

	Jazz	Hip-Hop	Rock	Classical

What is Miguel's favorite kind of music? _____ hip-hop
What is Anna's favorite kind of music? _____ jazz
What is Tran's favorite kind of music? _____ classical
What is Lisa's favorite kind of music? _____ rock

178. Katy's binder is square and has Katy's name and stripes on the front.

179. Seth is seven and his brother is four.

180.

D	C
A	B

181. The sea lion does not belong because it doesn't start with the letter "b."

183. ☐

184.

	Outfield	Pitcher	Catcher	First Base
Miguel				
Anna				
Tran				
Lisa				

Which position does Miguel play? _____ first base
Which position does Anna play? _____ pitcher
Which position does Tran play? _____ catcher
Which position does Lisa play? _____ outfield

185. Liza's magic wand is long and has a star on the end.

186. 2006

187.

C	A
D	B

188. The dinosaur does not belong because it is the only animal that is extinct. The others are endangered.

189. ⬭

190.

	Ice Cream	Candy	Cookies	Cake
Miguel				
Anna				
Tran				
Lisa				

What is Miguel's favorite dessert? _____ cookies
What is Anna's favorite dessert? _____ cake
What is Tran's favorite dessert? _____ ice cream
What is Lisa's favorite dessert? _____ candy